McLeod, John

Narrative of a voyage in his majestys late ship Alceste to the Yellow Sea

McLeod, John

Narrative of a voyage in his majestys late ship Alceste to the Yellow Sea

Inktank publishing, 2018

www.inktank-publishing.com

ISBN/EAN: 9783747781067

Wm Barthrop—

NARRATIVE

OF A

VOYAGE,

IN

HIS MAJESTY'S LATE SHIP ALCESTE,

TO

THE YELLOW SEA,

ALONG THE

COAST OF COREA,

AND THROUGH ITS

NUMEROUS HITHERTO UNDISCOVERED ISLANDS,

TO THE

ISLAND OF LEWCHEW;

WITH AN ACCOUNT OF HER

SHIPWRECK IN THE STRAITS OF GASPAR.

BY JOHN M'LEOD, SURGEON
OF THE ALCESTE.

PHILADELPHIA:
PUBLISHED BY M. CAREY AND SON,
Corner of Chesnut and Fourth streets.
1818.

ADVERTISEMENT.

The author of the following pages has attempted to narrate (in the best and shortest way he can) the occurrences of a voyage rendered remarkable by a combination of extraordinary events, and the circumstance of a communication with an interesting people, with whom, for the first time, Europeans have had any intercourse; and he has ventured a few occasional remarks, precisely as they arose in his mind on the spot, and which more mature reflection has not induced him to alter. He is aware that his thoughts, as well as his mode of expressing them, may be liable to comment; but he hopes that those who are mighty in criticism will be merciful in censure, and not visit with asperity that which is humble in pretension.

VOYAGE OF H. M. S. ALCESTE

TO

CHINA.

THE British government, on the representation of the court of directors of the East India Company, respecting the trade with China, having decided, with the view of relieving that branch of its commerce from the increasing vexatious impositions of the local authorities of Canton, on the measnre of sending an embassy to the court of Pekin; as on a former occasion of a similar kind, a distinguished nobleman had been selected to fill the situation of embassador extraordinary from the king of Great Britain to the emperor of China, who carried out with him a numerous suite composed of gentlemen well skilled in every branch of natural knowledge, with many curious and costly presents; so it was now determined to leave nothing short that could contribute to the splendour and respectability of the present embassy. The

B

right hon. lord Amherst (who had already filled the high situation of embassador to the court of Sicily) was appointed to conduct this difficult and delicate mission. Mr. Henry Ellis (formerly employed in a successful negociation with the king of Persia) was named secretary of embassy, with dormant powers to act as minister plenipotentiary, should any accident to the embassador render that circumstance necessary. The hon. Jeffery Amherst, as page; Mr. Hayne, as private secretary; Mr. Abel, as surgeon and naturalist; the rev. John Griffiths, as chaplain; Mr. Havell, as artist; and Dr. Lynn, with Mr. Maurige, Mr. Poole, and some others to fill the respective departments, constituted the suite of his excellency*.

Many valuable presents, supplied, as on the former occasion, by the East India Company, for the emperor and his ministers, consisting of specimens of our improved manufactures, made by the first hands, were also prepared. The command of the naval part of the expedition was intrusted to captain Murray Maxwell; and the Alceste, a frigate of forty-six guns, was fitted up for the reception of the embassador and suite. His majesty's brig Lyra,

* Lieut. Cooke, of the royal marines, was also attached to the embassy, on its landing in China, the guard being selected from that corps. Messrs. Abbot, Martin, and Somerset, were likewise added to it at this period.

commanded by captain Basil Hall, and the General Hewitt, Indiaman, by captain Campbell, accompanied the Alceste, the latter carrying out the presents.

On the 9th of February, 1816, the ships sailed from Spithead, and soon cleared the Channel, with a favourable breeze, which continued with us to Madeira, where we arrived on the 18th. In Funchal road we found the Phaëton, having sir Hudson and lady Lowe, with their suite on board, in their way to St. Helena ; and the Niger, with Mr. Bagot, on his mission to America. Our stay here was only twelve hours, and, in the evening, we pursued our course to the south-westward. The weather becoming hourly warmer, our people, who had been badly clothed, and had suffered a good deal from the severity of the cold in fitting out the ship, now began to thaw a little : things were beginning to find their proper places in the ship ; and those unaccustomed to the rolling motion had, by this time, acquired their *sea-legs*. On the 4th March, in the evening, at the moment of crossing the equinoctial line, the voice of some one, as from the sea, announced himself as Neptune's eldest son, and, after putting the usual interrogatories, added, that his father being a little indisposed, and rather *squeamish* about exposing himself to the night air, had deferred his visit until the morning, when he would personally call on board to inspect the strangers who were now entering his dominions. The son of Neptune seemed now to sink again into the deep. In the morning, his godship, agreeably to promise, appeared, seated in his car (a gun-carriage), with his trident and other insignia, attended by Amphitrite, and all his usual train of inferior deities. He was received by a strange-looking guard of his own, the band striking up "*Rule Britannia!*" After paying his respects to the embassador, the captain, and the rest, the novices, of whom there were not a few, were forthwith shaved, according to a practice immemorial, with a rusty iron hoop, full of notches; and the lather being washed off, by playing the fire-engine in their faces, they were then wiped dry with a dirty swab. Much mirth and good humour prevailed; and a double allowance of grog finished the ceremony. We experienced none of the calms usual near the line, and nothing of moment occurred until we reached the lat. 20° 4′ north, long. 31° 52′ west, on the 16th March, when the Lyra and Hewitt were directed to make the best of their way to the Cape of Good Hope, whilst the Alceste proceeded to the capital of the Brazils, where we arrived on the 21st of that month.

All the bold, as well as beautiful, features of nature, have conjoined to enrich the scenery of Rio Janeiro. The luxuriant descriptions of former travellers are by no means exaggerated, for it would indeed be difficult to exceed the truth in portraying the sublimity and grandeur of such a scene as presents itself on entering the harbour. The numerous islets appearing on this extensive sheet of water,—its richly-wooded banks, rising like an amphitheatre on either hand, studded with villages and country seats,—added to the distant view of lofty and picturesque mountains,—form, altogether, a very unusual and noble landscape.

The death of the queen, which happened the day previous to our arrival, at the good old age of eighty-two, had rather cast a gloom over the city of St. Sebastians. The batteries and ships fired five-minute guns during the whole day and night; the Alceste, Indefatigable, and a Spanish frigate, following this example; displaying also the usual exterior marks of grief, by hoisting the colours half-staff high, and topping the yards. The officers also wore crape; and, from a positive order being issued to all the inhabitants to go into mourning (which none dared, under the severest penalties, disobey), the prices of all black articles felt a sudden and enormous increase.

The government of the Brazils seems perfectly despotic; and it is painful to see even Englishmen lose the natural freedom of their character under such dominion. Some, who from long residence had imbibed the feelings of the Portuguese, would, in answering any question relative to public affairs, look cautiously around, to see who was near them, and then whisper their reply.

The prince (now the king), during the period her majesty lay in state, was shut up, according to their usage, not to be seen by any but his chamberlain.

Swarms of priests occupied every avenue to the palace, and hung in clusters on the staircases. St. Sebastians seems to be a soil, in which these members of the *autos da fé* still thrive well. The Brazils have lately been raised from the state of a mere colony to the dignity of a kingdom; and the residence of the court has conferred still more substantial advantages on it, arising from the emigration of the chief nobility from Portugal, and the transfer of their wealth to this country.

Its commerce has of late years increased to a great degree, chiefly, however, under the direction of English houses. The return of the court to the mother country, it is thought, would be the signal of revolt; for it is not probable the Brazils would long remain in their present fettered state, whilst colonies in all directions around them are freeing themselves from the oppression of the mother country. The want of the usual public attentions of saluting the flag of a foreign power might have been accounted for under the present circumstances of the court; but it was singular (considering, more particularly, our late relations with Portugal) that a house for the accommodation of the embassador and suite, during their short stay, and which had been granted to the former embassy, should have been refused in the present instance. The hospitality, however, of Mr. Chamberlayne, the British minister here, amply supplied this deficiency. All places of public amusement were of course shut; and the only *spectacle*, during our stay, was the funeral of the queen, which took place by torchlight; all the military that could be collected, both horse and foot, lining the streets (which were illuminated) from the palace to the convent of Ajuda. The herse and state-coaches were drawn up at the grand entrance, covered with black cloth, and near them the chief mourners, who were eight of the nobles, on horseback. Their dress was the ancient Portuguese costume of mourning. Each had a large broad-brimmed hat, rather slouching down upon the shoulders; a long black cloak, or robe, with the star of some order affixed to it; conveying to the mind of an English spectator the whimsical combination of a coal-heaver, a priest, and a knight. The king, accompanied by the two elder princes, attended the coffin to the principal porch, and saw it deposited in the hearse, when the whole cavalcade drove off, and the body was interred in the convent, with the usual religious ceremonies. The royal family next day appeared at the balconies of the palace; on which occasion it is usual for the Portuguese to stand uncovered in the square opposite; and, if any of the royal carriages are met on the road, the passengers on horseback must dismount, and even kneel.

Neither of their Portuguese majesties can themselves be considered as *regular beauties;* but the princesses are good figures, and certainly, upon the whole, handsome women. Don Pedro, their eldest son, promises to be a man of some spirit. Much indolence seems to exist among the inhabitants, and they are said still to possess their characteristic contempt of all reading; so that a publisher of books in the Brazils would probably earn but a lean livelihood. This country produces all the various fruits of the warmer climates; such as pine-apples, oranges, limes, mangoes, guavas, melons, bananas, &c.: the tea-shrub still continues to be an article of growth, under the direction of some Chinese accustomed to manage it; and it is to be hoped they may succeed in extending and improving its cultivation. The slave-trade still exists to its fullest extent; and this class of the population, however useful they may be, are certainly not ornamental; being the ugliest race of negroes that can be collected from the African coast—Gaboons, Congos, and Angolas. Our West-India islands having been generally supplied with Fantees, from the Gold Coast, with Eyeos, and Ashantees, who are a much finer-looking people; this circumstance, added perhaps to their improved condition, their better clothing, and general treatment, gives a slave of Jamaica a far less degraded appearance than one in this country. Yet, though the situation of the former is much ameliorated (and undoubtedly superior to his native state in Africa), it is unfortunate that the first European settlers of colonies, had not, instead of hunting down and oppressing the natives, trained them to habits of industry; when the term *slavery*, so revolting to humanity even under the most favourable circumstances, so contrary to reason and natural right, need never have been known. Our East-India possessions, and late occupation of Java, sufficiently demonstrate the practicability of this system.

They do Buonaparte, here, the honour of being very much afraid of him; and keep a bright eye to windward, lest he should break adrift from St. Helena, and come down upon them before the wind. This silly appearance of fear is something like the weakness of ordering his name never to be mentioned, than which, perhaps, nothing tends more to keep up his consequence.

This part of the Brazils is naturally hot during the months of December, January, and February; but (more especially as the southern are found to be comparatively colder than corresponding northern latitudes) it enjoys, during our summer, a sort

C

of tropical winter, and is not considered an unhealthy climate.

The town of St. Sebastians, without any public edifice worthy of notice, is regularly built, and, from the late influx of inhabitants, is daily extending its limits. Although this country produces plenty of beef, yet, from want of care and management, it is such as would be considered carrion in England; and in few parts of the world is there less accommodation for travellers, there being only some *casas*, or inns, of the most wretched description.

The Brazils display an inexhaustible field for the researches of the naturalist, for no where else can the objects of his inquiry be more varied or multiplied. The state of society here is represented, by those whose long residence and close intercourse afford them the means of judging, as extremely demoralized. The men, in their exterior appearance, are a squalid, *hysterical*, grim-looking set; but the ladies, though generally little, and dark-coloured, are not deficient in beauty or expression of countenance; they want, however, that elegance of gait and graceful walk, peculiar to the Spaniards. They are said to be more attentive to the external forms of decorum than to the essential practice of modesty; but this, if true, may "depend," as was suggested by an elegant writer of the last embassy, "on the example of the men;" for it would scarcely be reasonable to expect the perfection of female morals, where every manly virtue is unknown. At least three-fourths of the world are in a state of barbarism, where women have no character at all; being either immured in seraglios, or the mere slaves and play-things of their savage lords; but in that portion of it, which has a claim to civilization, where they are allowed to have minds, and assume their just rank, the slightest glance will shew, that among those nations where honour, intelligence, and worth, are held in most esteem by the one sex, they are uniformly rewarded by corresponding good qualities in the other.

The ship having recruited her supply of very excellent water*, and other matters settled, we took our leave of the American shore on the 31st of March, steering south-easterly until we got from 36° to 39° south, where we found the prevailing westerly winds. Keeping in the usual track for ships crossing the Southern Atlantic, we passed the islands of Tristan d'Acunha, about fifty miles to the northward of them. The wind continuing

* Captain Cook complained of the water here being very bad.—At that time, perhaps, the aqueduct was not so extensively covered, and secured from the admission of impurities, as at present.

favourable, we saw the Table Mountain on the 18th of April, and anchored on the same day in the bay. We arrived at a gay time, in the middle of horse-racing and balls. An India fleet touched here, homeward bound, one of the ships having on board the countess of Loudon and family, on the passage to England. Cape Town has now become almost an English place, and is too well known to require any description here.

As strangers, on first landing here, we were forcibly struck by the remarkable difference of complexion in the female part of the society, compared with the *brunettes* we had just left at Rio Janeiro; and an Englishman is probably the more inclined to esteem the beauty of the Cape ladies, from its great resemblance to that which he is accustomed to admire at home. It is hinted, however, that this resemblance exists chiefly during youth, and that, in their maturer years, they are apt (from sedentary habits and want of exercise) to acquire a *peculiar Hottentotish* obesity. But this, perhaps, is only said by ill-natured people.

The ship having gone round to Simon's Bay, and the necessary refitment being completed, his lordship embarked at this place, with the usual marks of attention, on the 6th of May, and we proceeded on our voyage. From 38° to 40° south, we found our expected winds; but, as winter was far advanced in this hemisphere (latter end of May, and beginning of June), the weather was cold, bleak, and boisterous, with a heavy sea. On the 24th May we made the islands of St. Paul and Amsterdam. Smoke was seen, as we approached, issuing from the crevices of the latter. It is here where the hot springs so nearly adjoin to the great salt water basin, as to afford the singular exhibition of catching fish in the latter, and boiling them in the former, without taking them off the hook, and within reach of the rod. The state of the weather, which was very rough, and the time of the evening, did not allow us to verify this fact, but there is no doubt of its truth. An immense crater (now apparently converted into a sort of harbour, the sea having flowed into it) appears on the eastern side of the island.

Having got sufficiently to the eastward for the purpose of fetching Java with the usual tropical winds, we began to hawl to the northward and eastward, the weather of course becoming daily warmer; and, on the 8th June, we saw Java Head, and anchored next day in Anjeri road, where we found the Lyra at anchor, and saw the Hewitt off Cape Nicholas, on her way to Batavia, they having only arrived two days before us*. This passage

* The superior sailing of the frigate enabled us to touch at Rio Janeiro, without in any way delaying the general passage; as, notwithstanding this, she nearly overtook her con-

was extraordinary for its rapidity, for in ninety-two days, under sail, the ship had traversed about fourteen thousand miles, and visited every quarter of the globe.

After staying a day or two at the village of Anjeri (where we were amused with the ceremony of a Javanese wedding), colonel Yule, the resident of the Bantam district, accompanied by Mr. M'Gregor, waited on the embassador to pay their respects; and having provided the necessary accommodation for his lordship and suite to proceed over land to Batavia, they all set out on their journey thither. During our short stay here, the king, or sultan, of Bantam, died; and his uncle (the nearest heir to the sovereignty) refused to accept the title, preferring to live in humble retirement. The Alceste, having completed her water, sailed also for Batavia, as she had brought out duplicate despatches for the evacuation of the island of Java. The Lyra, in the mean time, had been sent on to China, with a communication from lord Amherst to Sir G. Staunton.

On the 21st June we sailed from Batavia, with the general Hewitt; saw the island of Lucepara on the 23d, and entered the straits of Banca. Our

sorts at the Cape. The same was the case here, though she remained ten days behind, being able to afford them, in such a run, a start of 1000, or 1500 miles.

voyage up the China sea presented nothing unusual. On the 9th of July we met his majesty's ship Orlando, and received intelligence of the motions of our coadjutors at Macao. We joined them at anchor near the Grand Lemma on the following day, and found along with the Lyra, the Discovery, and Investigator, two surveying-ships belonging to the company, having on board Sir G. Staunton, and some other gentlemen* belonging to the factory, whose knowledge of the Chinese language rendered them necessary as interpreters.

The apparent reason of choosing this rendezvous, was to be free from the impertinence of the Canton official people, whose business it naturally was to thwart the measures, and throw every possible impediment in the way of, the embassy. Circumstances occasioning the delay of a day or two, the ships passed on to an anchorage among the Hong Kong islands; where the Anjeri water, not being deemed good, was changed for that which fell from the rocks, and was certainly uncontaminated by any vegetable matter, for few places present a more barren aspect than these islands. They are also called the Ladrones, from being the haunts of pirates; and for such a purpose their situation is ex-

* Messrs. Morrison, Manning, Toone, Davis, and Pearson.

tremely well adapted. Here a message arrived, stating the emperor's pleasure that the embassy should be received as in the former case; and that the necessary orders had been sent to the ports of the Eastern and Yellow Seas for that purpose.

On the 13th July the squadron (four ships and the brig) sailed; and, coasting along the provinces of Quang-tung and Fokien, passed through the straits of Formosa, and entered the Tung Hai, or Eastern Sea. The breeze altered its direction occasionally, but was always favourable; and, passing out of sight of the Chusan islands, we saw the land to the eastward, which we *then* conceived to be the south-west point of Corea. On the 24th we made Staunton's island, and capes Gower and Macartney, on the south-east part of the Shantong promontory; and, the next day, rounding close the north-east point, we entered the gulph of Pe-tche-lee. The country here had an extremely rugged and sterile look. On the 26th we passed through the Mee-a-tau islands, and steered for the mouth of the White (or North) River*, despatching the Lyra a-head, to announce the approach of the squadron.

An address was now publicly read by lord Amherst, to all the individuals who were to be attend-

* It is doubtful whether Pei means white or north; most probably the latter.

ants on the embassy, touching the great necessity of maintaining the strictest regularity and propriety of conduct in their intercourse with the Chinese, so as to avoid every cause of offence or disagreement; and laying down general regulations for their conduct in all respects.

We anchored, on the 28th*, not many miles distant from the mouth of the river; but the land is here so very low, that the mast-heads of the junks in the river, and the tops of the houses only of the village of Ta-coo, were visible from the ship. It would appear that the ships had entirely outstripped the expectations of the Chinese; for they had no idea of seeing them so soon, or that they should not have heard of them in their passage up. Such rapidity of movement never entered into their conceptions; for they, in fact, had scarce heard of them at one end of their empire, when they found them at the other.

The viceroy of this province (Pe-tche-lee) had been for some offence dismissed from his office; and his successor having not yet left Pekin, it was not until the 4th Aug. that two duly-authorized mandarins of rank (Chang and Yin) came on

* During our passage up the Yellow Sea the weather was remarkably serene and fine, and we experienced none of the fogs which usually hang over the shallower parts of the ocean.

D

board to pay their respects to the embassador, and to give the necessary directions for the disembarkation of the presents. To those who had seen, for the first time, the Chinese costume, these mandarins had a very strange appearance.—On a back view, their short jacket, or gown, with their crape petticoats, gave them the look of bulky old women; but, in confronting them, their clumsy boots and "beards forbade the interpretation." The fishermen in this vicinity (almost within a hundred miles of the capital) were literally naked,—even without a fig-leaf. This sort of indecency we were little prepared to meet, amongst a people who affect to be so *outrageously* decorous as to discourage the art of sculpture, because it displays too distinctly the shape and lineaments of the human body.

Chang was a civil, Yin a military, mandarin; and they had, as usual, the title of ta-zhin (or great man) added to their names. They were saluted on approaching the ship with seven guns each, and received with a guard. Every body was in full dress; and it could not be said of this, as of the last embassy, that there was any want of splendour in this respect. After a conference, in some degree ceremonious, and partly for arranging future proceedings, they partook of a banquet in the captain's cabin, and then returned to the shore. Quang, the chin-chae, imperial commissioner, or legate (as he has been variously termed), holding a superior rank to either of the others*, being ready to receive the embassador on shore, his lordship and the gentlemen of the embassy took their leave of us for a while, landing in great state on the 9th of August; the squadron being dressed in colours, the standard flying, the yards manned, and a salute of 19 guns fired from each ship. They proceeded into the river attended by a number of Chinese junks, and by our boats in regular order. During the time we remained at this place, presents of bullocks, vegetables, rice, tea, and other refreshments were, according to usage, sent off to the ships, but by no means in great abundance. Several of the bullocks were brought along-side dead, having been drowned in the bottom of the boats, or died otherwise in their passage off. This, however, was not meant as disrespect or incivility, for they make no distinction themselves between an animal that is killed by the butcher, and one which dies naturally; and in this way they eat dogs, cats, rats, and, in fact, all manner of carrion and vermin.

* The person holding such an office as this, *under the great seal*, obtains a kind of temporary rank, entitling him, for the time, to take precedence even of the viceroy of a province, although he may have an inferior button or ball on his cap, and be a mandarin of lower order in the state.

In this respect, therefore, they made no strangers of us, for they gave us their own family fare.

It was now determined, by the senior officer, that the Lyra, attended by the Investigator, should take a southerly direction in the gulf, whilst the Alceste and Discovery were to proceed to the north, a certain rendezvous being pointed out for our meeting again, to which the General Hewitt was also directed.

On the 11th we weighed, and stood to the north-eastward; the Discovery in company: the Lyra and Investigator to the southward. On the 13th saw the Sha-loo-poo-tien islands, extending from north-west by north to west by south, distant about five leagues. We coasted along the western shore of the gulf of Lea-tong, hitherto unexplored by any European ship; and found the land, as we advanced, became more and more mountainous. About noon, on the 14th, in latitude 39° 29′ N. longitude 120° 6′ E., the great wall of China opened to the view, bearing north-west by west, its nearest and lowest point being then distant about six or seven leagues; but we approached it closer in the afternoon.

Rising from the sea, this immense barrier passed over the first or lowest hill, and, mounting the second, was seen stretching to the right, in our point of view, obliquely towards its summit: then, on the third and still higher land, it inclined to the left, making an angle with the last range; and, ultimately ascending the highest and most distant mountain, it was there lost*. The opportunity of surveying this extraordinary structure, which, for more than twenty ages, has been deemed one of the greatest wonders of the world, afforded, more especially in this unexpected way, from the deck of a British man of war, the most pleasing sensations. Whether it is considered (as it is by some) a mighty effort of human industry, or (as by others) a monument of laborious folly, still it is an amazing object, not only from its immense extent, but on account of its great antiquity; and, from being so seldom visible to an European eye, to have beheld it, even at this distance, was a high gratification of curiosity. Beyond the wall is a remarkable head-land, very much resembling Cape Sicie, *a notorious place*, near Toulon. The wind heading us here, we stood across, about sun-set, toward the coast of Chinese Tartary; and on the 15th, in

* It extends for about fifteen hundred miles, and is carried equally over mountains and rivers.—" It is said not to be more than five-and-twenty feet high, flanked with towers at short distances, but of sufficient breadth for several horsemen to travel easily abreast. Report says, that one-third of the men in China, capable of labour, were employed in its construction, and that it was finished in the space of five years."

the evening, anchored in a bay* sheltered by winds from the north-west to south, but open to the southward and westward, lat. 39° 33′ N., long. 121° 19′ E. We found here a cascade of water gushing from the rock, which was excellent.

The natives, who most probably had never seen any ships of our class before, crowded down next morning on the beach, but shewed no inclination to come on board. Indeed the people here seemed to be less amphibious than those generally found on sea-coasts; few fishing or other boats were to be seen, although a very large and fine harbour, for vessels of twelve or fifteen feet water, extended inland round a point from the head of the bay.

The first officer who wandered up to the villages, about two miles from the watering place, was nearly devoured by the curiosity of the inhabitants. Being seated beneath a tree, every part of his dress underwent the strictest scrutiny, from the shirt-frill to the shoes; but the anchor-buttons seemed most to attract attention, for they would refuse a dollar, and gladly accept a button, for any thing. The women here had, universally, small feet, all who were seen (and on the *first morning* every woman in the village made her appearance) being crippled. This we by no means expected

* Named Ross Bay.

to have found so far on the Tartar side of the great wall.

But these people are, in fact, completely Chinese; the language, dress, and religion of that country evidently prevailing: and they appear to differ in no material respect from those we afterwards saw in the province of Shan-tong, except that they were less rude and uncivil. No public officer, or man of any rank, made his appearance to inquire into the motives of our arrival. They were remarkably neat in their houses and gardens; and there was an air of comfort about their villages, not always to be found in the more civilized parts of Europe. The face of the country is mountainous, and extremely denuded of wood; not a tree being visible, except in the immediate vicinity of their dwellings. The hills had the appearance of sheep-feeding downs in England; and the soil, as far as we could penetrate, was excellent, and a good deal cultivated; the *holcus sorghum* appearing a prominent object.

Many deep fissures or gulleys were observed on the sides of the mountains, occasioned by the torrents from the melting snow in summer; for, although this part of the country is in the same parallel as the north of Italy or south of France, and was now (in August) very warm, yet the wintery season must be extremely cold, from the general situation and appearance of the country, and the bleak winds blowing over the uncultivated wilds to the northward of it. The rocks here were composed of a very ponderous sort of stone, evidently containing a great proportion of iron; and some slate was observed. There must be some town of commercial importance situated at the head of the gulf, from the number of junks we saw passing up and down. Some matchlocks were noticed at this place, but they were merely in the hands of individuals, as fowling-pieces; for no military made their appearance. We were unable to procure a supply of fresh beef;—not from want of cattle; but they could not comprehend the value of Spanish dollars, this coin of such universal circulation being melted down, the moment it gets into the hands of a Chinese of Canton.

Having completed our water, we weighed on the 19th, and steered along-shore to the southward. At four in the afternoon, we saw a considerable town, lying in a hollow between two red cliffs, the neighbourhood immediately around being rather fine, and better wooded than usual. It seemed a place of some trade, and a number of junks were lying at anchor in the roads. The narrow promontory which here extends into the Yellow Sea, and forms the eastern boundary of the gulf of Lea-tong, was, from its resemblance to a sabre, named the Regent's Sword: the south end of it is the extreme Tartar point, and was called Cape

Charlotte, in honour of her royal highness the princess.

Leopold's Isle lies a little to the north-west of this cape.

The coast along this shore from our anchorage was not unlike that from Plymouth Sound to the Start. Next morning (20th), steering southerly, we passed through a cluster of islands (nearly opposite and not very far distant from the Mee-a-taus), which were named the Company's Group. The space between them and Cape Charlotte, St. George's Channel; that through which we had sailed, Leadenhall-Passage; Ried's Rock and Grant's Island were names appropriated on this occasion. Soon after we saw the Mee-a-tau islands; and, in the afternoon, passed the city of Ten-cheu-foo, at which lord Macartney, in the last embassy, touched. It looks very well from the sea, but the wall seems of much greater extent than is necessary for the town. Stood on to the eastward, and entered, in the evening, the bay or harbour of Kin-san-seu or Zew-a-tau. The clear and accurate description of it, by sir Erasmus Gower, enabled the Alceste to proceed in without the least hesitation or difficulty. Here we found the General Hewitt. There are two towns on the peninsula, forming the north-west side of the harbour, and one on the opposite shore. They have no fortifications here; at least none deserving that name. The people ap-

E

peared a gross and boorish set, and we enjoyed the *happiness* of being crowded with them from day-light till dark, when they always went away without the least expression of thanks for civilities shewn them. We here noticed that all the females, high and low, had small feet, which is by no means the case in the southern provinces, especially about Canton. At the latter place, among the middling and lower classes, the feet are allowed to remain in their proper state, unless the girl promises to be handsome, in which case she is crippled, in order to give the finishing touch to her beauty, and with the view of preparing her for the mandarin market, where small feet bring a higher price, and she occasionally, also, obtains some interest or favour for her parents through the connexion.

They walk, or rather totter along, like one shuffling on her heels only, without putting the fore part of the foot on the ground; and in moving quick, they not unfrequently tumble down, when they must get up again the best way they can; for Chinese gallantry was never observed to extend so far as to afford any help on such an occurrence. Some, more cautious, were seen to move about, supporting themselves by the walls of the houses. Girls, from early infancy to eight or nine years old, were carried about in arms, their feet being too tender, during the first years of this absurd and cruel operation, to enable them to bear their weight;

the four smaller toes being turned down under the sole, the whole foot and ancle cramped, and the growth impeded by tight bandages, and a small shoe, which is generally again enclosed in a larger one. The pain and irritation excited by this horrid process, as well as the want of exercise, evidently injures their general health, for all the female children had a sickly pallid look. It would be as difficult to account for the origin of this barbarous practice, as that of squeezing the waists of English women out of all natural shape by stays (an usage which has not long been laid aside); or of "treating men like mere musical instruments," and *tuning* them, as such, in Italy.

On shore the people were inhospitably rude, and even the children were encouraged to be insolent, and to throw stones. One mandarin seized a basket of vegetables from the officers' steward, ordering him and the interpreter (whom he also beat) into the boat, with a number of opprobrious epithets, such as "Foreign Devils! Spies!" &c. Our relation with the embassy tied our hands at this time.

Finding no refreshment was to be obtained here, and being told, by some one in authority, that there was a greater probability, of getting cattle at another harbour, forty miles farther to the eastward, we prepared to proceed thither.

We had by this time been joined by the Lyra; captain Hall having surveyed the western and southern shores of the Gulf of Pe-che-lee, which were found to be in general low. One place, remarkable for its height over the adjoining land, had been named Mount Ellis. Here we parted for a time with our worthy friends of the General Hewitt, the companions of our voyage outward; that ship proceeding to Canton, to complete her ulterior objects. On the 26th we weighed from Zeu-a-tau, and next morning arrived at Oie-aie-oie, a very extensive and secure harbour, the Lyra sounding the passage in. On our entrance a number of mandarins (or, as the seamen termed them, *mad marines*) came on board to pay their respects; and an old turret on the face of a hill fired three popguns by way of salute, turning out about a dozen and a half of soldiers, who looked a good deal like the stage-military in an old-fashioned play.

Their salute was returned by an equal number of guns from the ships. Here died Mr. Gawthrop, the master, aged forty-three years, (thirty-three of which he had been to sea,) after a severe illness contracted at the Cape of Good Hope. He had been distinguished as a good seaman and correct navigator; his career in the navy had also been marked by his abilities as a surveyor of coasts and harbours; and, although a man of blunt manners, his honesty was sterling. The ship's reckoning had been kept, during his confinement, by Mr. Taylor, the chaplain.

We buried him at sea, near the mouth of the harbour, with military honours; it not being considered right to inter him among a set of men who would have disturbed the grave for the coffin or the clothes, and of whose thievish disposition we we had had the fullest example. We lost no time at this place, where nothing substantial was to be found*, but proceeded to sea on the 29th, standing to the eastward along the Shan-tong shore. On the 31st we saw the land bearing east; but, the wind being light, anchored in forty-three fathoms. Towards morning we weighed, and the next day anchored again among a cluster of islands, lat. 37° 45′ N., long. 124° 40′ 30″ E. on the coast of Corea. The natives here exhibited, by signs and gestures, the greatest aversion to the landing of a party from the ships, making cut-throat motions by drawing their hands across their necks, and pushing the boats away from the beach; but they offered no serious violence. These islands were named Sir James Hall's Group; the main land, of considerable height, was in view, and not far distant. Weighed again, and, the wind being northerly, stood to the southward. On the 2d we

* Here parted for Macao the Discovery and Investigator. They were towed up, and sailed down again.

were out of sight of any land; but, the wind changing to the eastward, made sail southerly, and, on the 3d, passed a number of islands, with which the sea was studded as far as the eye could reach from the mast-head; and, on the 4th, stood into a fine bay formed by the main land to the northward and eastward, and sheltered in a great degree in other points by Helen's and other islands to the westward; and anchored in six fathoms in front of a village, a larger town being observed at some distance. In the evening six or seven large boats came off to the Lyra (being nearest the shore), having on board a chief (most probably of this district), attended by a numerous retinue. There he met the commodore; and, after partaking of some refreshment, proceeded, although it was now dark, on board the Alceste. He was saluted, on leaving the Lyra, with three guns, which was repeated by the frigate. As he shoved off from the brig, one of his attendants, having in some way or other misbehaved, was by his order extended on the deck of the boat, and received, in a summary way, about a dozen and a half of blows with a flat bamboo over the seat of honour; and, as the culprit squalled, a number of his companions standing round him joined in the howl, either in derision, or to drown his noise. This ceremony finished, a flourish of trumpets and other instruments announced his approach to the frigate. He was a man apparently about seventy years of age, of a very venerable and majestic mien; his hair and beard of a hoary whiteness. His dress was a light blue robe, with loose sleeves, and fastened round his middle by a buff-coloured leathern girdle. He had on his head an immense hat, not less than five or six feet round the brim, made of some substance resembling horse-hair varnished over. The cavity to receive the head being fixed *under the brim*, that which rose above it, as in European hats, was not larger than a common tumbler. He wore a kind of half-boots, very much peaked and turned up at the points; and in his hand he held a short black stick, twisted round with a silken cord, which seemed to be the badge of his office. Divested of his broad-brimmed hat, he would not upon the whole have made a bad representative of old *king Lear*. Of his attendants some were military, being distinguished by a short sword or rapier, the officers wearing peacocks' feathers in their hats (a distinction which also exists in China for men of merit): and the rest were civilians. He was ushered into the cabin, where, in preference to chairs, he sat down upon one of the sofa-cushions, placed upon deck. It appearing to be etiquette for the head to be covered, the whole party, consisting of captains Maxwell, Hall, and other officers, conformed to this rule, and, squatting on the cabin-floor, with gold-laced cocked hats on, amid the strange costume of the Coreans, looked like a party of masquers.

Much edifying conversation was no doubt lost on this occasion; for much was said, but unfortunately not one word was understood, the Chinese interpreter we had on board not being able to write his own language; and some of the Coreans could write, although they could not speak, at least, that dialect which he comprehended. The old gentleman, however, displayed, by signs, his satisfaction at the mode of his reception; and, after partaking of some liqueurs and sweetmeats, took his departure late in the evening from the ship, when he was again saluted, his band striking up one of their martial airs.

During the night several boats were anchored near the Lyra, apparently to watch her motions; and early in the morning the same chief, accompanied by a still greater retinue, was seen embarking at the nearest village, and soon after he visited the Lyra, where he breakfasted. He had in his train some secretaries (or men of letters), who employed themselves in noting down every thing relative to the ships which could be acquired by signs: the complement of men was described by pointing to them, and then, holding up ten fingers a certain number of times; they counted the guns, examined the muskets, measured the decks, &c. &c. A shot was fired, by express wish, from one of the carronades; and the distance it went, but particularly its *recochetting* along the surface of the water, seemed to strike them with astonishment. After breakfast, a small party of the officers (captains Maxwell, Hall, Messrs. Clifford, Law, and M'Leod) got into the boats with the view of landing at the village; and the old chief, thinking they were going to the frigate, accompanied them, his own boats attending. But no sooner did he perceive the course directed to the shore than his countenance fell, and he seemed altogether in a state of great perturbation, making signs that he wished to go to the Alceste, and shaking his head when they pointed to the town.

Having reached the beach, the party landed, and were immediately surrounded by a concourse of people. The old chieftain hung his head, and clasped his hands in mournful silence; at last, bursting into a fit of crying, he was supported, sobbing all the way, to a little distance, where he sat down upon a stone, looking back at the officers with the most melancholy aspect. His feelings appeared to be those of a man who imagined some great calamity had befallen his country in the arrival of strange people; and that he was the unhappy being in whose government this misfortune had occurred.

The natives, who had in the mean time been driven by their soldiers to a respectful distance,

F

stood gazing in astonishment alternately at their afflicted chief and at our party.

Captain Maxwell, seeing what distress it occasioned him, would permit no advance, and, beckoning to him to come back, he arose, and slowly returned.

It was explained as well as could be done that no injury was intended, and that we were friends. He pointed to the sun; and, describing its revolving course four times, he drew his hand across his throat, and, dropping his chin upon his breast, shut his eyes, as if dead; intimating that in four days (probably the period in which an answer could arrive from Kin-ki-tao, the capital, for he also pointed to the interior) he would lose his head. One of his secretaries, or legal advisers (an amazing long-winded man), squatted on the top of a large stone, now made a harangue of considerable length, the purport of which was evidently against the advance of the strangers. Signs were made for something to eat and drink (thinking hospitality might induce them to invite us into their houses); but messengers were instantly despatched to the village, who brought down little tables, with mats to sit on, and some refreshments: this, however, not being the object, they were not accepted, making them understand that it was unbecoming to offer them in that unsheltered manner, on the open beach; and, by way of a hint that this was not *our* mode of treating strangers, invited them to return to the frigate, where they should dine handsomely, and meet with every respect. The old man, who had observed attentively, and seemed perfectly to comprehend the meaning of the signs, answered by going through the motions of eating and drinking with much appearance of liveliness and satisfaction, patting his stomach afterwards, to say all was very fine; then, looking grave, he drew his hand across his neck, and shut his eyes; as if to say, "What signifies your good dinners when I must lose my head?"

Perceiving it was impossible to penetrate farther into the interior without violence, which we had neither the right nor the inclination to use, the party re-embarked, *affecting* to be much hurt at the treatment they had received.

The old gentleman followed on board the Alceste, seemingly much dejected, and looking as if ashamed that he could not pay more attention. Wandering about the decks, attempting to converse, by signs, with every one he met, he took a piece of paper from a gentleman who was sitting at his desk, and wrote some characters upon it, which he seemed to require an answer to, but of course none could be given. The paper was retained; and, being shewn some months afterwards to Mr. Bannerman, at Canton, turned out to be, "I don't know who ye are; what business have ye here?"

It was pretty evident, however, that he was acting from orders which he dared not trifle with, rather than from any inhospitable feeling in his own nature.

He received a Bible, which captain Maxwell (to whom he seemed very thankful for not insisting upon going into the town) presented him with, and carried it on shore with much care, most likely supposing it to be some official communication.

Basil's Bay (which this place was named) lies in lat. 36° 9′ N., long. 126° 32″ E., being, in sea-phrase, about 120 miles *high and dry* up the country, according to the existing charts.

This afternoon (5th) got under weigh, and stood to the southward, through innumerable islands, which were all high, rising like mountains out of the sea. None of them seemed of great extent, few appearing longer than three or four miles, and, as far as we could see, in some degree cultivated, the inhabitants generally crowding to the top of the highest eminence, where they remained huddled together, and gazing until the ships were passed.

On the 8th, anchored in lat. 34° 26′ N., and here we found that the land seen on coming up the Whang Hai or Yellow Sea, and which had been called Cape Amherst, was not the continent. It was now named Alceste Island; and another range, about twenty in number, running north and south, rather within it, but outside the Corean Archipelago, was called the Amherst Isles. This morning, after sounding our way in, came to an anchor in a most excellent harbour, named Murray's Sound; the two islands, which principally form it, Shamrock and Thistle.

Here a number of observations were taken, and surveys made, to ascertain the exact geographical position of the land, and the qualities of the anchorage; and distinguishing names were of course given to remarkable spots, which might serve on future occasions as leading marks. From the top of Montreal, one of the highest, 135 other islands were distinctly counted; the main land, which seemed very lofty, was seen ranging from north-east to east-south-east, distant about forty miles. From Murray's Sound, Craig Harriet, a very peculiar rock, rising in sugar-loaf form from the sea, bears south 39°, west five miles. Another rock (Huntly Lodge), situate on an island, south 40° east, resembles a church with a square tower. Windsor Castle, north 40° 50′ east. The direction of the sound itself north north-east half east, and south south-west half west; it is a very secure anchorage, with excellent holding ground. The intervening spaces between the multitude of isles, generally from one to two, or three, and even four miles across, are all (at least as far as the boats examined) close harbours, and capable of containing, in security, all the navies of the world. They form, in fact, an almost endless chain of harbours, communicating with each other. The rise and fall of tide is here considerable, but the setting of the currents among such a multitude of isles must, of course, be extremely various. They appear to be all inhabited, and therefore must possess fresh water. On first landing on Thistle Island, the women fled, with their infant children, over the hill, to a place which we named Eagle Point (from a large eagle being perched on the precipice as we came in), and hid themselves in recesses among the rocks; whilst the men, in a body, but unarmed, waved and hallooed to us not to advance, making the usual signal with their hands across the throat. When they found, however, by repeated visits, that no hostility was intended, and that we were rather inclined to give than to take from them, they became a little more tame, would crowd round the officers to see them fire at a mark, bring them water to drink, and offer them part of their humble fare to eat; but all this they seemed to do in a perfect spirit of independence, and not from fear. Then suddenly, as if recollecting they were acting contrary to orders in holding any correspondence whatever with strangers, they would lay hold of some of the gentlemen by the shoulders, and push them away, pointing to the ship; and this conduct was uniform wherever we touched. We observed

no fire-arms among them, but some who came on board the Alceste discovered considerable acquaintance with the sword exercise. They cultivate as much grain as they want for their own consumption; they feed cattle (at least for domestic purposes); and, as may naturally be supposed, from their peculiar and insular situation, they subsist a good deal by fishing. Of their government, general manners, and customs, it would be impossible to speak with any accuracy from so limited an intercourse as we had with them.

China has very little communication with *the barbarians of the west*, and that is chiefly confined to a particular spot, the port of Canton; Japan still less, and Corea none at all. A connexion, however, is kept up with China by two or three annual junks from the eastern coast.

What little knowledge we possess of Corea is mostly derived from the Jesuits of China, who certainly were not infallible guides in *all matters*; but in the geography, general literature, and delineation of manners and customs, when unconnected with their own superstitions, their labours are entitled to a distinguished place in the republic of letters, especially when the difficulties they had to struggle with are taken into consideration; but here they were freed from every motive to deceive, and had only to tell the simple truth.

Corea (or Kaoli) is tributary to the emperor of China, and sends him triennial embassadors expressive of its homage. We saw enough, however, to convince us that the sovereign of this country governs with most absolute sway; and that, occasionally, he makes very free with the heads of his subjects. The allusion to this danger could not have been so constant and uniform, in places so remote from each other, without some strong reason.

The law against intercourse with foreigners appears to be enforced with the utmost rigour*. At one of the islands, to the north, where we first landed, a Corean, in an unguarded moment, accepted a button, which had attracted his attention; but soon after, as the boats were shoving off, he ran down into the water, and insisted on restoring it, at the same time (by way of reparation) pushing the boat with all his might away from the beach. On almost all occasions they positively refused every thing offered to them. His Corean majesty may well be styled "king of ten thousand isles," but his *supposed* continental dominions have been very much circumscribed by our visit to his shores. Except in the late and present embassy,

* It is said that the crew of a Dutch vessel, a considerable time since, wrecked on the eastern coast, were detained in slavery for nineteen years, without being heard of, when some of them managed to get away.

Alceste's Voyage.

To Face Page 40.

J. Hill Sc.

no ships had ever penetrated into the Yellow Sea; the Lion had kept the coast of China abroad only, and had neither touched at the Tartar nor Corean side. Cook, Pérouse, Bougainville, Broughton, and others, had well defined the bounds on the eastern coast of this country, but the western had hitherto been laid down on the charts from imagination only, the main land being from a hundred to a hundred and thirty miles farther to the eastward than these charts had led us to believe.

The Jesuits, therefore, must have taken the coast of Corea from report, and not from observation, for their chart is most incorrect, and by no means corresponds with their usual accuracy. The Chinese written characters have found their way here, but they would appear to be confined to the literati, for the common language has no resemblance in sound to the colloquial language of China.

On the tenth we got under weigh and proceeded on our voyage, standing through the south passage, and made sail to the southward, giving the name of Lyra to an island which bore about east of Alceste's ten or twelve leagues, and distance nearly the same north-westerly from Quelpart. On the 11th, sounded in forty-nine fathoms muddy bottom, in lat. 31° 42′ N., long. 126° 30′ E. On the morning of the 13th we made Sul-

G

phur Island, a volcano, situated in lat. 27° 56′ N., long. 128° 11′ E. Whilst yet at a great distance, we could observe a volume of smoke at short intervals bursting from its crater. We hove-to for some time under its lee, in front of a horrid chasm, from whence the smoke issued, but found it impossible to land, as there was much wind and swell, and the surf broke with tremendous violence around its base. The island, which does not appear above four or five miles in circumference, rises precipitously from the sea, except in one or two spots; its height must be considerable, judging from the distance we saw it, perhaps 1200 feet. The sulphurous smell emitted, even when two or three miles off, was very strong. One end of the island displayed strata of a brilliant red-coloured earth, which had been noticed before on some part of the Corean main. One would almost be induced to believe that the mercury and sulphur, so abundant in these regions, had combined to give this vermilion hue to the ground. From hence we stood on to the southward with a strong wind at north by east, which soon increased to a gale. Not having sufficient run for the night, and being totally unacquainted with the coast we were approaching, the ship was put under snug canvas, and hauled to the wind on the starboard tack. On the morning of the 14th we again made sail, and soon observed an island rising like a cone to a considerable height, with that of the grand Lewchew* immediately behind it. The state of the weather would not warrant our standing closer in with the land than about eight miles, as it now blew fresh from the west-north-west, which made it a lee shore. We hauled to the south-westward, and in the afternoon saw breakers under our lee, the Lyra being closer in, and rather a-head. To have put about with the wind as it then was, would have embayed us for the night; for the main body of the island seemed to form, with the peak we had left astern, and the position we were now in, a sort of bight. The Lyra, indeed, could not have tacked in such a swell, and was almost too near to attempt wearing. Both ships, therefore, stood on with every sail they could carry, on the starboard tack, endeavouring to weather the reef. Much anxiety existed, at this moment, on board the Alceste, for the fate of the brig; the breakers rearing their white tops close to leeward of her, and rolling, with terrific force, upon the rocks. By steady steerage, however, and a press of sail, she at last passed the danger, and bore up through a channel formed by the reef and some high islets to the southward, very much to the satisfaction of all concerned; and she was followed by the frigate.

* Generally termed Lekeyo in charts.

We hove-to, for the night, under the lee of the larger island, and the next morning's dawn, the weather being now extremely fine, displayed to our view a rich extent of cultivated scenery, such as we had not been lately accustomed to, on the naked coasts of Tartary and China. Rising in gentle ascent from the sea, the grounds were disposed more like the finest country-seats in England than those of an island so remote from the civilized world,—the tranquil, placid, and refreshing look of every thing around, forming a very pleasing contrast with the boisterous sea and dangerous condition of the previous day. We were in front of a town, having a sort of line wall along the water's edge, from whence some fishing-boats approached the Lyra, which by this time had anchored; and on the people being interrogated, by signs, as to the proper anchorage, they pointed round the south-west end of the island, kindly offering, at the same time, some vegetables and fresh water, which they had in their canoes.

We made sail in the direction indicated, carefully sounding and looking out as we advanced along shore, and at night anchored in eighty-two fathoms. On the 16th, at day light, we continued our course, and about noon descried a considerable town, with a number of vessels at anchor under it, in a harbour, the mouth of which was formed by two pier-heads. In the afternoon, having explored our passage through the adjacent reefs (the Lyra leading), we anchored in front of this town. The astonished natives, who most probably had never been visited by an European ship before*, were perched in thousands on the surrounding rocks and heights, gazing on the vessels as they entered. Soon after, several canoes came alongside, containing some people in office, who wished to know to what country we belonged, and the nature of our visit. By the assistance of the Chinese interpreter, whose language some of them understood, they were informed that we were ships of war belonging to the king of England, which had carried an embassador from that monarch to the emperor of China; and, after having landed him and his retinue near Pekin, we had, on our return to Canton, where the embassador was to re-embark, met with violent weather at sea, in which the ship had sprung a leak, obliging us to put in there, in order to repair our damages. To make this story feasible, the well was filled by turning the cock in the hold; and the chain-pumps being set to work, threw out volumes of water on the main deck, to the great amazement of these people, who seemed to sympathize very much with our misfortunes.

* Captain Broughton, after the loss of the Providence in 1797, anchored at this place in a schooner, and remained forty-eight hours.

This *ruse* was necessary to free their minds from that state of alarm, which must naturally arise on the arrival of ships of such unusual appearance and force, with whose motives they were unacquainted, and who would justly be considered as the objects of suspicion, had no reason but mere curiosity been assigned. They returned on shore, and put in requisition a number of carpenters, or people acquainted with the construction of their own vessels, who, at daylight in the morning, hurried on board, bringing with them the rude implements of their art, in order to render what assistance they could in stopping the leak. This offer of kindness was, of course, civilly declined by the senior officer, on the ground that we had plenty of good carpenters on board, who were perfectly equal to the task; that an asylum was all we required during the time of repair, with permission to take on board some fresh provisions and water, of which we stood much in need; and all this we would most cheerfully pay for.

An immediate supply of bullocks, pigs, goats, fowls, eggs, and other articles, with abundance of excellent sweet potatoes, vegetables, fruit then in season, and even candles* and fire-wood, followed this intimation; supplies of the same description

* Their candles are made of unrefined wax, with paper wicks, and give an excellent light.

being sent on board as often as was necessary, for about six weeks, the period of our stay on the island; those who brought them taking a receipt to shew they had been delivered safely; but the chief authorities, who sent them, obstinately refusing any payment or remuneration whatever.

Meantime, it being found impracticable for the frigate to swing in the inner harbour at low water, the road in which we lay was accurately examined, and found to be so protected with coral reefs to seaward, and covered by the land to the eastward, as to be completely sheltered, except in a very slight degree at its entrance, and of sufficient extent and depth to contain even ships of the line.

On the 20th, we moved up to the head of this road, to a place which we called Baron-pool, where we afterwards rode out the equinoctial gales (or change of the monsoons).

On inquiring of them where the king was, they said, after some hesitation, 10,000 miles off; and when it was hinted that it was necessary to have a party on shore, such as ropemakers and smiths, where they could have more room to work, and thereby expedite our refit; they requested this might not be done until they heard from the king, it being an unprecedented case, in which they were incompetent to act without orders.

Unwilling to give cause of alarm or uneasiness to a people who seemed so well disposed, and for whose fears and suspicions it was but reasonable to make every allowance, we remained quietly on board until the 22d, when intimation was received that a great personage intended paying a visit to the commodore.

At the mouth of a little river, in front of which we were anchored, we observed this chief embarking amidst a great concourse of people. He was saluted on his approach with three guns from each ship, and received on board with every mark of respect. He was a man about sixty years of age, with a venerable beard: his dress a purple robe, with very loose sleeves, and fastened round his middle with a sash of red silk: he had sandals on his feet, with white gaiters, not unlike short stockings. His cap (the badge of his dignity) was made of some slight material, twisted neatly into folds, and covered with a light purple-coloured silk. He had a numerous suite with him; some were official people of different ranks, and the rest his personal attendants. Here the occasion of our visit was again discussed; the pumps were set to work to shew the effect of the leak; and promises, on their part, renewed, of every assistance.

Although they had not heard from the king on the subject of our coming on shore, and notwithstanding it was contrary to a general rule for any stranger to land upon their coast, yet a few of the officers were always welcome to walk about within certain bounds. After partaking of a very handsome entertainment, he took his leave, the captain promising to return his visit. At one o'clock on the following day the boats were manned, and captains Maxwell and Hall, with several of the officers, in full uniform, proceeded into Napa-kiang*. This harbour is the mouth of a river, at the entrance of which, on each side, are strong-built walls or piers, for a considerable way up, and inside were anchored several rather large junks. Vessels under the size of frigates could be received very well in this river;—the bottom is soft mud. The river widens somewhat immediately above the anchorage, and in it is situated a very pretty little island. At the landing-place the party were met by some of the chiefs, who had been most in the habit of visiting the ships, each of whom, taking one of the officers by the hand, led him through an immense collection of spectators to the gate of a public building, where the old gentleman already mentioned attended to welcome them into the house. Here an entertainment was served up in

* Napa appears to have been the original name of the town; but, since their connexion with China, the term Foo, (or city of the first class) has been added; making Napa-foo. Kiang, another Chinese word, signifies river, and, when coupled with Napa, means merely the river, port, or anchorage of the place.

a style, which a pastry-cook, or connoisseur in eating, might describe; but which to another might be a difficult task. The utmost good humour, however, prevailed, and a liqueur (chazzi) something like rosolio was passed round in abundance, so that it was quite a man's own fault if he was not cheerful.

Many loyal and friendly toasts, applicable to both countries, were given and drank with enthusiasm. As they had hitherto generously supplied the ships with fresh provisions, vegetables, and fruit, and constantly refused any kind of payment, either in money or by way of barter, the captains thought this a proper opportunity to offer, as a mark of their personal regard, some presents to the chiefs, consisting of various wines, cherry brandy, English broad cloths, a telescope, and other things; and on this ground only they were accepted; reserving it to themselves, at the same time, to make what personal return they might think proper to this interchange of friendship.

At the end of this conference, when it was proposed to take a walk over the city, a consultation was held among them; when the request was mildly declined (supposed to be through the influence of *Buonaparte*, a man of dark and peculiar aspect, so named because he was suspected of being the most inclined to keep us at arm's length), stating, they were afraid some bad people might be induced to treat us with disrespect. It was evident they had not the power, without higher authority, to admit us to freer access; for the people themselves, almost without exception, appeared by this time to have no apprehension about our motives. After much hilarity the party took their leave, attended in the same way as on landing.

It was worthy of notice how much regularity and decorum existed among so many thousands as were here collected. A lane was formed, on the inner side of which the smallest boys (generally kneeling) were placed; another row squatted behind these; then the men (those nearest stoooping a little); and outside the still taller people, or those mounted on stories, &c.; so that all, without bustle or confusion, might have a complete view of the strangers. The utmost silence reigned, and not a whisper was heard. Perhaps they had purposely sent their women out of the way,—but the ladies managed (as usual) to outwit them, and to gratify curiosity in defiance of every precaution to the contrary. A number of them had either been placed intentionally on the other side of the river, or left there in consequence of all the men having come over to *the show;* but the boats, in going out, had to pass within a few yards of *their* pierhead; when, finding themselves in almost exclusive possession of that bank, they left their station on a hill, ran down to the point, and had their peep, whilst their friends on the opposite shore were unable (had it been their intention) to keep them in the back ground.

About this period a mutual friendship began to exist between us; confidence took place of timidity; and now, instead of permitting only a few to visit the shore at a time, they fitted up the garden of a temple as a general arsenal for us: the habitations of the priests were allotted as an hospital for the sick, whilst other temporary buildings of bamboo were erected for the reception of our powder, which required airing, and for various stores wanting inspection and repair. The rope-makers, smiths, and other artificers, were established at a convenient spot, about a mile farther along the beach. They continued their usual supplies, bringing us even fresh water on board in their boats; and, understanding we required some wood for spars, they felled fir-trees, floated them down the river, and towed them alongside, singing their usual boat-song, which had a very plaintive and pleasing effect.

The island of Lewchew* is about sixty miles

* It is called by an infinity of names in books and charts, such as Lekeyo, Lieoo-Kieoo, Lequeyo, and Lieu-Kieu; but the word Lewchew will better express the sound, according to the native pronunciation, than any other. It is often by the lower classes corrupted into *Doo-Choo.*

long and twenty broad; Napa Kiang, our position (and within five miles of Kint-ching, the capital), lying in lat. 26° 14′ N., long. 127° 52′ 1″ E. This is its south-west point, the main body of the island extending from hence north, a little eastwardly.

It is the principal island of a group of thirty-six, subject to the same monarch, and the seat of the government. The natives trace their history back to a period long anterior to the Christian era; but their first communication with the rest of the world, when their accounts became fully corroborated and undisputed, was about the year 605, when they were invaded by China, who found them at that time—a time when England and the greater part of Europe were immersed in barbarism—the same kind of people they are at the present day, with the exception of a few Chinese innovations; or, at least, they appear to have altered but in a very slight degree. Indeed, it is very obvious that a revolution in manners, and alteration of habits, are by no means so likely to occur with a people thus living in an obscure and secluded state, as among those who have a wider intercourse with other nations. The only connexion which the Lewchews have had with their neighbours, and that but very limited, has been with Japan and China, from neither of whom they were likely to receive any example of change.

The clearest and perhaps the only account given of their history is by Su-poa-Koang, a Chinese doctor or philosopher, who was, in 1719, sent as embassador to them*. The following is the substance of his report as to their origin:—"The Lewchew tradition states, that, in the beginning, one man and one woman were produced in the great void or chaos. They had the joint name of Omo-mey-kieou. From their union sprang three sons and two daughters; the eldest of the sons had the title of Tien-sun, or Grand-son of Heaven, and was the first king of Lewchew; the second was the father of the tributary princes; the rest of the people acknowledged the third as their progenitor†. The eldest daughter had the title of Celestial Spirit; the second, the Spirit of the Sea. After the death of Tien-sun, twenty-five dynasties reigned successively in this country, occupying (according to their story) a period of 17,802 years previous to the time of Chuntein, who commenced his reign in 1187. This is their fabulous history, of which they are very jealous; but nothing certain was known until 605, before which the inhabitants of Formosa and the adjacent islands were denomina-

* Vide Lettres Edifiantes, tome xxiv.

† It seems rather unaccountable, in this marvelous tradition, that the third son, to whom no wife is assigned, should have had the most numerous progeny.

ted by the Chinese *the Oriental Barbarians.* In this year the emperor sent to examine them; but, from want of interpreters, no clear account was obtained. They brought back, however, some of the islanders to Sin-gan-foo, the capital of the province of Chensi, and the seat of the court under the Souy dynasty. Some Japanese, who happened to be there, knew the people, and described them as a race of barbarians. The emperor Yang-ti sent forthwith some who understood their language to Lewchew, to command their homage, and acknowledgment of him as their sovereign. The prince of Lewchew haughtily replied, that he would own none as his superior. A fleet with 10,000 men was now fitted out from Amoi and the ports of Fokien, which force, overcoming the efforts of the islanders, landed at Lewchew; and the king, who put himself at the head of his people to repel the enemy, being killed, the Chinese burned the capital; and, carrying off 5000 of the natives, as slaves, returned to China. From this, until 1291, the Lewchews were left unmolested, when Chitsoo, an emperor of the Yuen family, reviving his pretensions, fitted out a fleet against them from the ports of Fokien; but, from various causes, it never proceeded farther than the western coast of Formosa, and from thence returned unsuccessful to China. In the year 1372, Hong-ou, emperor of China, and founder of the Ming dynasty, sent a great mandarin to Tsay-tou, who governed in Tchon-chan, the country being at this period divided, in consequence of civil disturbances, into the three kingdoms, who, in a private audience, acquitted himself with such address as to persuade the king to declare himself tributary to China, and to request of the emperor the investiture of his estate.

"Having thus managed by *finesse* what arms had been unable to effect, the emperor took care to receive, with great distinction, the envoys sent by their master. They were accompanied by offerings of fine horses, scented woods, sulphur, copper, and tin, and sent back again with rich presents for the king and queen; among which was a gold seal.

"The two kings of the other districts, Chan-pe and Channan, followed the example of Chonchan, and their submission was most graciously received. Thirty-six Chinese families were sent to live in Cheouli*, where grants of land were conceded to them; here they taught the Chinese written characters, introduced Chinese books, and the ceremonies in honour of Confucius. The sons of the Lewchewan grandees were also sent to Nankin to study Chinese, and were educated with distinction, at the expense of the emperor.

* That district of Tchon-chan in which the capital is situated, and where we resided.

"The reigns of Ou-ning and Tse-chao, the son and grandson of Tsay-tou, presented nothing extraordinary; but that of Chang-pa-chi was marked by the reunion of Chan-pe and Channan with Tchon-chan into one kingdom, and the government has since continued in the hands of a single chief. Lewchew is said henceforth to have had considerable intercourse with China and Japan in the way of commerce, *much to her advantage*, and to have even mediated between those two powers when misunderstandings had occurred.

"The famous Tay-cosama, however, emperor of Japan, whom the Chinese call ambitious, piratical, irreligious, cruel, and debauched, because he had pillaged their coasts, sent a haughty letter to Chang-ning, commanding him to transfer his homage from China to Japan, which Chang-ning as firmly refused. Notwithstanding the death of Tay-cosama, the Japanese fitted out a fleet at Satsuma, made a descent on Lewchew, took the king prisoner, and carried him off, having plundered the palace, and killed one of his near relations, who also resisted the acknowledgment of the Japanese. During a captivity of two years, Chang-ning acquired the admiration of the captors by his unyielding firmness and constancy in refusing to swerve from his first allegiance, and they generously sent him back to his states.

I

"The Tartar dynasty, soon after this, was placed by conquest on the throne of China, and made some alteration in the nature of the tribute to be paid, stipulating that envoys, in future, should be sent to Pekin only once in two years. Chang-hi paid much attention to the welfare of Lewchew; and his memory to this day is much respected by the people. It is said to be nearly a thousand years since the bonzes of the sect of Fo introduced their mode of worship into these islands, which has continued to the present time.

"When they take an oath, it is not before the statues or images of their idols; but they burn incense, and placing themselves in a respectful attitude before certain consecrated stones which are to be seen in various public situations, they repeat some mysterious words, said to have been dictated by the divine daughters of Omo-mey-kieou. They have also among them a set of holy women, who worship certain spirits deemed powerful among them, and who visit the sick, give medicines, and recite prayers. This seems to have given rise to the accusation of an old missionary at Japan, who said they practised sorcery and witchcraft. Chang-hi likewise introduced among them the adoration of a new deity, under the name of Tien-fey, or Celestial Queen. Polygamy is allowed here as in China, but seldom practised. Men and women of the same surname cannot intermarry. The king can only take a wife from one of three great families, who always hold the most distinguished posts: there is also a fourth, of the highest consideration, but with which the princes cannot form an alliance, because it is doubtful whether that family is not itself of the royal line. Their chiefs are generally hereditary, but not always; for men of merit are promoted, and all are liable to be degraded for improper conduct. The king's revenue arises from his own domains; from imposts on salt, sulphur, copper, tin, and several other articles; and from this income he defrays the expenses of the state, and the salaries of the great officers.

" These salaries consist nominally in a certain number of bags of rice; but they are paid generally in silks, and various other necessary articles of clothing and food, in proportions equal to the value of so many bags of that grain. All their interior commerce or marketing is performed by the women and girls at regulated times. They carry their little loads upon their heads with singular dexterity, consisting of the usual necessaries of life and wearing apparel, which they exchange for what they more immediately want, or for the copper coin of China and Japan*. The men are said to be neat workmen in gold, silver, copper,

* We saw no money among them.

and other metals; and there are manufactories of silk, cotton, flax, and paper. They also build very good vessels, quite large enough to undertake voyages to China and Japan, where their barks are much esteemed. They have adopted the Chinese calendar with respect to the division of the month and year. This island produces rice, wheat, and all sorts of vegetables, in abundance. The people of the coast are expert fishermen, and the sea and rivers are well furnished with fish. They are famous divers, and obtain shells and mother-of-pearl, very much esteemed in China and Japan.

" They possess many woods proper for dyeing; and one tree in particular yields an oil which is held in great repute. They have likewise a great variety of most delicate fruits, oranges, citrons, lemons, *long-y-ven*, *lee-tchees*, grapes, &c. Wolves, tigers, and bears, are unknown; but they have many useful animals, such as horses, water-dogs, black cattle, stags, poultry, geese, peacocks, pigeons, doves, &c.

" The camphor, cedar, and ebony, are among the number of their trees; and they have also wood well fitted for ship-building, and for public edifices. They are represented as disdaining slavery, lying, and cheating. They are fond of games and amusements, and celebrate, with much pomp, the worship of their idols, at the end and commencement of the year; and there exists much

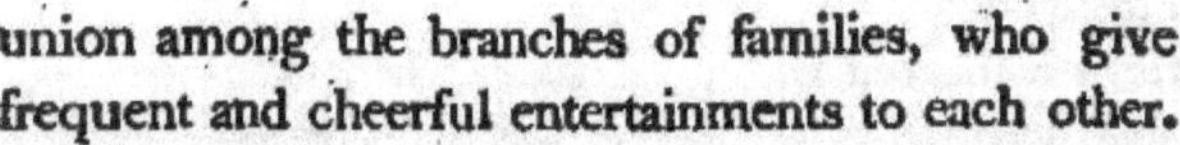

union among the branches of families, who give frequent and cheerful entertainments to each other.

The ceremony of installation of the king of Lewchew is thus described: "When the king dies, his heir sends an ambassador to the emperor, to make known that circumstance, and to demand his investiture.—Meantime the Lewchews treat as king and queen the prince and the princess his wife, though it is not, according to the Pekin regulations, until after the installation that they assume the titles. The emperor either sends from himself a qualified person to perform this ceremony, or grants full powers to the Lewchew embassador to do so on his return.

"If the former is determined upon, the emperor orders the tribunal of ceremonies to find a fit person to sustain with dignity the majesty of the Chinese empire; and the choice falls on whom they know the emperor wishes, a second being named in the event of death or sickness. The emperor, after approving the choice, admits the embassador to an audience, and gives them the necessary instructions, and the presents intended for the king and queen. The mandarins of Fokien are ordered to equip a vessel, and to choose a captain, officers, sailors, soldiers, and pilots, sometimes amounting to three hundred and fifty persons. The embassador is conducted from court with great pomp to the capital of Fokien, where he is lodged in a commodious palace, and treated with much distinction.

" He is embarked with great state, when, after the usual ceremonies to heaven, and the goddess Tienfey, they make sail. On their anchoring near Napa Kiang, the king gives the necessary orders for receiving the embassador, with all the honours due to the title of *Celestial Envoy*, that is, to the envoy of the son of heaven, or the emperor of China. The princes and grandees repair to the port in their court dresses. A number of vessels richly ornamented conduct the stranger into harbour, where the embassador and suite lands, and is attended to his palace with great pomp by the princes and grandees, who take care to make such an appearance as to do honour to the nation. Every thing is regulated with respect to the maintenance of the embassador and retinue, who are all permitted, even to the lowest domestic, the privilege of carrying a certain quantity of money, and of Chinese merchandise, *to make a little trade.* In the time of the Ming dynasty, the profits of the Chinese were considerable at Lewchew; at present only moderate. The embassador ordinarily piques himself on having no *personal* connexion with commerce*.

* This is quite in the inflated style of these *celestials*, whilst in the practice of every thing that is sordid.

Alceste's Voyage. To Face Page .62.

J. Hill. Sc.

" After having taken some repose, he repairs to the grand hall, where he finds a magnificent *estrade*, on which he seats himself. On a signal given, at the same instant, the princes, ministers, and grandees of the first order, placed according to rank, make the nine prostrations to salute the emperor. The embassador stands; and, after the ceremony, makes a profound reverence. When the chiefs of the second and third class prostrate themselves, he also stands, and afterwards presents his hand to them. On the performance of the inferior chiefs, the embassador is seated, but afterwards presents his hand to them. This ceremonial finished, some grandees on the part of the king come to congratulate the embassador on his safe arrival. The rest of the day is spent in repasts, public rejoicings, and concerts, in all the cities and neighbouring villages, and on board the vessels. On a certain day the embassador goes to the temple of the goddess Tienfey, to return thanks for her protection, and from thence to the imperial palace, where he performs the Chinese ceremonies, in honour of Confucius. On another day the embassador with all his retinue repairs to the royal hall, where are the tablets of the deceased kings, the heir to the throne also appearing, but as a prince simply.

" The embassador then performs, in the name of the emperor, the Chinese marks of respect in honour of the deceased king, the predecessor of the reigning prince, and also for his forefathers; and presents the odours, the silks, manufactures, and silver, sent by the emperor for that purpose. The prince then makes the nine prostrations to thank the emperor, and inquires after the state of his health. He next salutes the embassador, and dines, familiarly, and without ceremony, with him. When all is regulated for the instalment, the embassador with all his suite, and a great number of people, proceed to the palace. The court is filled with lords and chieftains, richly attired, and ranged in proper order. On his entrance, the embassador is received by the princes, and conducted, with music sounding, to the royal hall, where there is an elevated *estrade* for the prince and princess, and and a distinguished place for the embassador. All the princes, grandees, and ministers, standing, the embassador reads, with a loud voice, the imperial diploma; in which the emperor, after some eulogy on the defunct sovereign, acknowledges for king and queen the hereditary prince and princess his wife. This declaration is accompanied by exhortations of the emperor to the new monarch, to govern according to law; and to the people of the thirty-six isles to be faithful in their allegiance. After it is read, the imperial patent is presented to the king, who transfers it to the minister, to be retained among the archives of the court. Then the king, queen, princes, &c., make the nine prostrations, to salute and thank the emperor. The embassador next displays the rich presents from his master to the king and queen, when the usual thanks are returned. Whilst the embassador reposes himself for a short time in an adjoining apartment, the king and queen, seated on their thrones, receive the homage of the princes, ministers, grandees, and deputies, of the thirty-six isles. The queen then retires, and the king entertains the embassador with much splendour.

"Some days afterwards, seated in the royal chair, borne by many porters, the king, followed by the princes and ministers, and a brilliant suite, goes to the hotel of the embassador.

"The road is ornamented by triumphal arches; —and at certain distances are found tents, in which are placed fruits, flowers, and perfumes. Around the chair of the king are seven young girls, on foot, carrying his flags and umbrellas. The princes, ministers, and grandees, are on horseback, and are emulous to distinguish themselees, on this occasion, by their superb dresses and numerous suite.

"The embassador, at the gate of the hotel, receives his majesty with great respect, and leads him to the grand hall. The king now again salutes the emperor; after which he honours the embassador, by offering with his own hand wine and tea. This the embassador declines; and, re-

K

turning the cup, he takes one for himself, which he does not drink until after the king has first drank his. This ceremony finished, his majesty and suite return to the palace. He names, some days afterwards, an embassador to proceed to the court of the emperor, to thank his majesty, and to send him presents, a list of which is *communicated* to the Chinese embassador, and he orders a vessel to be equipped, which accompanies that of the Chinese on its return. At last, the imperial envoy, having determined the day of his departure, takes leave of the king; and some time afterwards the latter proceeds to the hotel of the embassador, to wish him a happy voyage, and to make the usual prostrations in honour of the emperor, and to return him thanks.

"During the sojourn of the embassador, the king gives him frequent entertainments; sometimes in the grand palace; at others in his pleasure-houses; and, occasionally, in water-parties. The queen, princesses, and ladies, assist at these ceremonies. They have music, dancing, and comedies, with songs, in praise of the imperial and royal families, and of the embassador, &c."

Such is the account of Supoa-Koang; and, having observed a great part of what he relates to be true, it is but fair and reasonable to give him credit for what we had not the opportunity of actually seeing. One thing appears very evident,—

that these poor islanders have been much cajoled and humiliated, as well as encumbered with a load of ceremonies, very foreign to their nature, by the usurpation of the Chinese.

The dress of these people is as remarkable for its simplicity as it is for its elegance. The hair, which is of a glossy black (being anointed with an oleaginous substance, obtained from the leaf of a tree), is turned up from before, from behind, and on both sides, to the crown of the head, and there tied close down; great care being taken that all should be perfectly smooth; and the part of the hair beyond the fastening, or string, being now twisted into a neat little top-knot, is there retained by two fasteners, called *câmesashee* and *usisashee*, made either of gold, silver, or brass, according to the circumstances of the wearer; the former of these having a little star on the end of it, which points forward. This mode of hair-dressing is practised with the greatest uniformity, from the highest to the lowest of the males, and has a very pleasing effect, whether viewed singly, or when they are gathered together. At the age of ten years the boys are entitled to the *usisashee*, and at fifteen they wear both. Except those in office, who wear only a cap on duty, they appear to have no covering for the head, at least in fine weather. Interiorly, they wear a kind of shirt, and a pair of drawers, but over all a loose robe, with wide sleeves, and a broad sash round their middle. They have sandals on their feet, neatly formed of straw; and the higher orders have also white gaiters, coming above the ancle. The quality of their robes depends on that of the individual.—The superior classes wear silk of various hues, with a sash of contrasting colour, sometimes interwoven with gold.—The lower orders make use of a sort of cotton stuff, generally of a chesnut colour, and sometimes striped, or spotted, blue and white.

There are nine ranks of grandees, or public officers, distinguished by their caps; of which we observed four.—The highest noticed was worn by a member of the royal family, which was of a pink colour, with bright yellow flowers.—The next in dignity was the purple; then plain yellow; and the red seemed to be the lowest.

On the female attire we could make but little observation.—The higher ranks are said to wear (and some indeed were seen with) simply a loose flowing robe, without any sash; the hair either hanging loose over the shoulders, or tied up over the left side of the head, the ends falling down again. The lower orders seemed to have petticoats scarcely deeper than a highlander's kilt, with a short, but loose, habit above.

The island of Lewchew itself is situate in the happiest climate of the globe.—Refreshed by the sea-breezes, which, from its geographical position, blow over it at every period of the year, it is free from the extremes of heat and cold, which oppress many other countries; whilst from the general configuration of the land, being more adapted to the production of rivers and streams than of bogs and marshes, one great source of disease in the warmer latitudes has no existence: and the people seemed to enjoy robust health; for we observed no diseased objects, nor beggars of any description, among them.

The verdant lawns and romantic scenery of Tinian and Juan Fernandes, so well described in Anson's Voyage, are here displayed in higher perfection, and on a much more magnificent scale; for cultivation is added to the most enchanting beauties of nature. From a commanding height above the ships, the view is, in all directions, picturesque and delightful.—On one hand are seen the distant islands, rising from a wide expanse of ocean, whilst the clearness of the water enables the eye to trace all the coral reefs, which protect the anchorage immediately below. To the south is the city of Nafoo, the vessels at anchor in the harbour, with their streamers flying; and in the intermediate space appear numerous hamlets scattered about on the banks of the rivers, which meander in the valley beneath; the eye being, in every direction, charmed by the varied hues of the luxuriant foliage around their habitations. Turning to the east, the houses of Kint-ching, the capital city, built in their peculiar style, are observed here and there, opening from among the lofty trees which surround and shade them, rising one above another in gentle ascent to the submit of a hill, which is crowned by the king's palace: the intervening grounds between Napafoo and Kint-ching, a distance of some miles, being ornamented by a continuation of villas and country-houses. To the north, as far as the eye can reach, the higher land is covered with extensive forests.

At a short distance from this eminence, the traveller is led by a foot-path to what seems only a little wood; on entering which, under an archway formed by the intermingling branches of the opposite trees, he passes along a serpentine labyrinth, every here and there intersected by others. Not far from each other, on either side of these walks, small wicker doors are observed, on opening any of which, he is surprised by the appearance of a court-yard and house, with the children, and all the usual cottage train, generally gamboling about; so that, whilst a man fancies himself in some lonely and sequestered retreat, he is, in fact, in the middle of a populous, but invisible, village.

Nature has been bountiful in all her gifts to Lewchew: for such is the felicity of its soil and climate, that productions of the vegetable kingdom, very distinct in their nature, and generally found in regions far distant from each other, grow here side by side. It is not merely, as might be expected, the country of the orange and the lime; but the banyan of India and the Norwegian fir, the tea-plant and sugar-cane, all flourish together. In addition to many good qualities, not often found combined, this island can also boast its rivers and secure harbours; and last, though not least, a worthy, a friendly, and a happy race of people.

Many of these islanders displayed a spirit of intelligence and genius, which seemed the more extraordinary, considering the confined circle in which they live; such confinement being almost universally found to be productive of narrowness of mind. Our friends here were an exception to the general rule.—*Madera Cosyong*, one of our most constant and intimate friends, acquired such proficiency in the English language, in the course of a few weeks, as to make himself tolerably understood. He evidently came on board, in the first instance, as a spy upon our conduct, before they were satisfied that we meant no harm; and no man was ever better adapted for this duty; for, as his conciliatory and pleasing manner won upon all hearts, he had therefore a natural access every where, and, had "stratagems or schemes" existed, he of all others was the most likely to have discovered them.

His not assuming his proper character, which was that of a man of some distinction, until his mind was satisfied about us, and his then doing it with frankness, is a proof that such were his original motives. To acquire our tongue, he marked the sound of any English word for the most familiar articles of the table, or terms of conversation, and noted them in symbols of his own language, with their signification, which enabled him, with slight reference to his vocabulary, to manage without having recourse to the interpreter. If he happened to be walking on shore with any of the officers, he would not lose the sound or meaning of a word because he had not his book with him, but scratched it on the leaf of a tree, and transcribed it at his leisure. His first attempt to connect a sentence was rather sudden and unexpected. Rising to go away one evening after his usual lesson, he slowly articulated, "You give me good wine,—I tank you,—I go shore."—He delighted in receiving information, and his remarks were always pertinent.—The map of the world, with the track of the ship from England to Lewchew, was pointed out and explained to him, which he, as well as others, seemed to trace with peculiar care, and at last, in a great degree, to comprehend, although the subject was, in the first instance, entirely new to them, for they certainly had no idea of the vast extent or figure of the globe.

He was gay or serious, as occasion required, but was always respectable; and of *Madera* it might be truly said, that he was a gentleman, not formed upon this model, or according to that rule, but "stamped as such by the sovereign hand of Nature."

They all seemed to be gifted with a sort of politeness which had the fairest claim to be termed natural; for there was nothing constrained, nothing stiff or studied in it.

Captain Maxwell having one day invited a party to dine with him, the health of the king of Lewchew was drank in a bumper:—one of them, immediately addressing himself with much warmth and feeling to the interpreter, desired him to state how much they felt gratified by such a compliment; that they would take care to tell it to every body when they went on shore; and proposed, at the same time, a bumper to the king of the *Engelees*. A Chinese mandarin, under the like circumstances, would, most probably, have *chin-chinned* (that is, clenched his fists) as usual; he would have snivelled and grinned *the established number* of times, and bowed his head in slavish submission to the bare mention of his tyrant's name; but it would never have occurred to him to have given, in his turn, the health of the sovereign of England.

This superiority of manner brought to recollection the boorishness of the Chinese near the Pei-ho.

L

Some mandarins, who were not of a rank sufficiently high to be entertained in the cabin, were invited to dine with the officers; and some of them, after gnawing the leg of a fowl, would without any ceremony thrust the remains of it into any other dish near them; and instead of following our example (as the Lewchews uniformly did) in pouring out the wine into glasses, or, indeed, in any way accommodating themselves to our style, they would take up, with both hands, the decanter, and applying it to their greasy mouths, thereby secure the exclusive possession of that bottle.

These islanders are represented as being remarkable for their honesty and adherence to truth, and to this character they appear to be fully entitled. The chiefs informed us that there was little probability of their stealing any thing; but, as iron implements were a great temptation, they begged that none might be left carelessly about.—Although, however, the rope machinery and other articles remained, for many nights, unguarded on the beach, and their opportunities on board were numberless, yet not one theft occurred during the whole of our sojourn among them. That proud and haughty feeling of national superiority, so strongly existing among the common class of British seamen, which induces them to hold all foreigners cheap, and to treat them with contempt, often calling them outlandish lubbers *in their own country*, was, at this island, completely subdued and tamed by the gentle manners and kind behaviour of the most pacific people upon earth. Although completely intermixed, and often working together, both on shore and on board, not a single quarrel or complaint took place on either side during the whole of our stay; on the contrary, each succeeding day added to friendship and cordiality.

Although it was, no doubt, infringing on their established rules for strangers to land upon their coasts, yet they granted every possible indulgence, and conceded the point as far as they could; for their dispositions seemed evidently at war with the unsocial law. When any of the officers wandered into the country beyond the bounds prescribed, they were never rudely repulsed, as in China or Morocco, but mildly entreated to return, as a favour to those in attendance, lest they should incur blame; and, as their appeal was powerful, it was never disregarded.

They erected little temporary bamboo watch-houses or sheds, where those engaged in this duty resided; and, as we wandered about, handed us over from one post to another. In these houses they always pressed the officers to partake of their fare, which was often very good, especially a kind of hung beef, which they have the art of curing extremely well.

They appear to be much accustomed to these pic-nic sort of parties, having a small japanned box, containing sliding drawers for the various viands, which a boy generally carried, on the end of a bamboo, to any part of the fields where they thought proper to dine.

One man, very often accompanied by *Geroo*, or (as he was sometimes termed, from having a constant smile upon his countenance) *the laughing mandarin*, seemed to carry about with him a constant supply of these refreshments, and chazzi, a liqueur, which led us to believe that he had been deputed for the express purpose of paying attention to our officers.

The sudden vicissitudes of weather to which we had been exposed, by leaving England during extreme cold, and passing suddenly into the torrid zone; then immediately afterwards into the cold raw climate of the southern Atlantic; meeting with heat again at the Cape of Good Hope; then crossing in rather a high latitude the chilly Southern Ocean; and, quickly following that, appearing on the burning coast of Java; might, in fact, be said to have exposed us, in the short period of four months, to the effects of three summers and three winters; and proved, as might naturally be supposed, extremely trying to the health of the men. On our arrival at Lewchew, our cases of sickness, though not numerous, were severe; and to the kindness of the natives may, in a great measure, be attributed their recovery. They were not only comfortably lodged, but the higher class of people* daily attended, inquiring into their wants, giving additional *coogas* or eggs, and other delicacies, to those whose cases more particularly required them, and paying a cheering attention to the whole; for theirs was a substantial, not a cold or ostentatious charity.

A young man, whose case had long been hopeless, died here. On that night a coffin was made by our own carpenters, whilst the natives dug a grave, in the English manner, in a small burial-ground under some trees near the landing-place.

Next morning we were astonished to find a number of the principal inhabitants clad in deep mourning (white robes with black or blue sashes), waiting to attend the funeral. The captain came on shore with the division of the ship's company to which the man belonged, and proceeded to the

* One elderly man, whom Mr. Fisher (the assistant surgeon), who was always at the hospital, thought to be a physician, wrote something at the desk, which Mr. Fisher concluded was a prescription. On translating it afterwards at Canton it turned out to be a moral maxim: "Let not the present day be passed in idleness.—The days of our youth will not return.—By being diligent and studious we arrive at offices of rank."—(Literally) "We ride on horseback, and wear embroidered clothes."

garden where the body lay. His messmates bore the coffin, covered with the colours; the seamen ranged themselves two and two, in the rear of it; next were the midshipmen; then the superior officers; and last of all the captain, as is usual in military ceremonies of this kind. The natives, who had been watching attentively this arrangement, and observing the order of precedence to be inverted, without the least hint being given, but with that unassuming modesty and delicacy which characterize them, when the procession began to move, placed themselves in front of the coffin, and in this order marched slowly to the grave. The utmost decency and silence prevailed whilst the funeral service was performing by the chaplain, although there was a considerable concourse of people; and afterwards they marched back, but in different order, to the garden. Here they took the directions for the shape of a stone to be placed at the head of a tomb, which, as a mark of respect, they had already begun to erect over the grave. This was soon finished; and the shape of the English letters being drawn with Indian ink, they, notwithstanding the simplicity of their tools, cut out with much neatness the following epitaph, which, when explained to them, seemed to be highly gratifying:—

Here lies buried
Aged Twenty-One Years, William Hares, Seaman,
Of His Britannic Majesty's ship Alceste.
Died Oct. 15, 1816.
This Monument was erected
By the King
And Inhabitants
Of this most hospitable Island.

The day after the interment they went to the tomb, with their priests, and performed the funeral service according to the rites of their own religion. There is not an act of these excellent and interesting people which the mind has not pleasure in contemplating and recollecting. Not satisfied with having smoothed the path of death, they carried their kind regards even *beyond* the grave!

Of our religion they could form no idea, nor was it possible to explain it to them. They seemed at first to consider us as worshippers of the sun or moon, and, of course, our astronomers as high priests, from seeing them busied about an observatory which had been erected in our garden, with a large telescope for the examination of the heavenly bodies.

One Sunday a number of them were observed, during divine service, peeping through the quarter-deck ports, but were not noticed in sufficient time to invite them in.

Captain Maxwell's horse, in riding one morning to inspect the progress of the artificers, stumbled, and fell among some rocks; and by this accident the fore finger of his left hand was not only fractured, but badly dislocated. Some of his Lewchewan friends, who were near him, ran to the next village for one of their surgical professors. He soon arrived, and, after much salutation, proceeded to examine the injury (the dislocation had in the interim been reduced by the coxswain pulling upon it), and then stated that he would come on board the ship, whither the captain was then proceeding, in an hour, with the applications he thought necessary for it. At the time appointed, one of the chiefs, with this surgeon, and another more in the character of a physician, and their retinue, some of them bearing a medicine-chest, made their appearance alongside. The injury being again examined (and it having been previously decided they were to have the management of the cure, under surveillance, in order to observe how they would act), a fowl was killed with much form, and skinned, and a composition of flour and eggs, with some warm ingredients about the consistence of dough, was put round the fractured part (which had the effect of retaining it in its position), and the whole enclosed in the skin of the fowl. As this fowl appeared to have been sacrificed, its skin being applied to enclose the whole was most probably meant to act as a charm.

The manual part finished, the physician proceeded to examine the general state of health, and the pulse appeared to be his chief, and indeed only guide in this respect. The arm was laid bare to the shoulder, and he applied his fingers with great attention, and with as much solemnity as ever issued from Warwick-lane, to the course of the artery, and at all parts of the arm where he could feel it beat, to ascertain whether it was every where alike; and, lest there should be any mistake in this point, the other arm underwent the same investigation; the whole party looking all the while extremely grave. Having now decided as to the medicines necessary on this occasion, his little chest was brought forward, with his pharmacopœia, and a sort of *Clinical Guide*, directing the quantity and quality of the dose.

His chest was extremely neat, its exterior japanned black, and a number of partitions in it, again subdivided, so as to contain about a hundred and eighty different articles (quite enough in all conscience, even among the greatest hypochondriacs and drug-swallowers); but they were fortunately all simples, being a collection of wood-shavings, roots, seeds, and dried flowers of his own country. There appeared also some ginseng, a product of Tartary and Corea, much in vogue in these parts. Small

M

portions of the specified articles were measured out with a silver-spatula, and put up in little parcels, and directions were now issued as to the mode of boiling and drinking the decoction. Next day they were highly delighted to hear the good effect of their medicines, though they had never been taken (as many a poor doctor is cheated by cunning patients); and a new application was brought for the finger, termed a fish poultice, so composed as to look, and indeed to smell, something like currant-jelly.

Having carried on this scheme for a few days, they were then informed that the finger was so much better as to render their attendance unnecessary any longer; and, as a reward for their services, they were presented with some little articles, and, among others, as an addition to the chest, some spirits of hartshorn, displaying to them its effect on the olfactory organs, with which they were quite astonished and pleased; some spirits of lavender and oil of mint, they also considered a great acquisition. The physician, more especially, seemed to be a very respectable man, and was treated as such by those about him. Their practice seems to be a good deal derived from the Chinese, for their notion of the circulation of the blood, or rather their having no correct notion about it, is the same. Neither have they any idea of anatomy from actual observation, and, of course, the greater operations cannot be undertaken; one man only was examined by Mr. Rankin, who had lost his arm, and his stump was rather a *rude one*. Some corn was left with them, which they promised to cultivate; and fortunately captain Hall had some English potatoes, which were likely to be productive, and the mode of planting them was particularly described. Their fields were extremely neat, and their furrows arranged with much regularity, by a plough of a simple construction drawn by bulls, assisted occasionally by the use of a hoe; and they practised irrigation in the culture of their rice. A young bull of English breed (though calved on the island) was presented to the chief authorities by captain Maxwell, leaving them also a cow (having two on board), so that it is possible the next visitors who touch at Lewchew may find a larger, though they cannot find a better, race of cattle.

The mode of dancing of these people may, strictly speaking, be termed *hopping*; for they jump about upon one leg only, keeping the other up, and changing occasionally, making a number of extravagant motions, and clapping with their hands, and singing at the same time their dancing song. According to our notions, this was their only ungraceful action. A number of them thus engaged, more especially when joined by the officers (who must needs acquire their style), formed rather a grotesque assembly. They attempted our mode of country dancing, and managed (considering it was necessary to make use of both feet) tolerably well.

The Lewchews are a very small race of people, the average height of the men not exceeding five feet two inches at the utmost. Almost the whole animal creation here is of diminutive size, but all excellent in their kind. Their bullocks seldom weighed more than 350 lb., but they were plump and well-conditioned, and the beef very fine; their goats and pigs were reduced in the same proportion, their poultry seeming to form the only exception. However small the men might be, they were sturdy, well-built, and athletic. The ladies we had no opportunity of measuring, but they appeared to be of corresponding stature.

These islanders, most probably, originated from Japan or Corea, having a good deal of the Corean lineaments, but rather milder, and softened down. They are obviously not of Chinese origin, having nothing whatever of that *drowsy* and elongated eye which peculiarly distinguishes the latter; nor would it seem that the few Chinese and their descendants settled on the island freely mixed with the native Lewchews, the national features and the natural disposition of the two people being perfectly distinct, and differing in every respect. Neither have they any mixture of Indian blood, being quite as fair as the southern Europeans; even those who are most exposed being scarcely so swarthy as the same class of society in Spain or Portugal.

The Chinese language is learnt by a few, as the French is in our own country; but the bonzes, who are also schoolmasters, teach the boys their native language, which is a dialect of the Japanese, and is rather soft and harmonious; and they have nothing of that hesitation in utterance, or appearance of choking, which is observed in the former, often requiring the action of the hands to assist the tongue*. The orders and records of government are in their own, or Japanese character; but they have books in the Chinese language.

They burn the bodies of their dead, and deposit their bones in urns (at least in our neighbourhood), in natural vaults, or caverns of the rocks along the sea-shore. The graves of the few Chinese residents here are formed in their own style.

Crimes are said to be very unfrequent among them, and they seem to go perfectly unarmed, for we observed no warlike instruments of any description; and our guns, shot, and musketry, appeared to be objects of great wonder to them. It must have been the policy of the Chinese to disarm them, for it appears that, in the first instance, they defended themselves nobly against their attacks, as

* In this respect the Chinese seem to resemble what is said of a Frenchman:—That if his hands are tied he cannot speak.

well as those of the Japanese. Not even a bow or arrow was to be seen; and, when they observed the effect of fowling-pieces in the hands of some of the gentlemen, they begged they might not kill the birds, which they were always glad to see flying about their houses; and if we required them to eat, they would send in their stead an additional quantity of fowls on board every day.—An order was immediately issued to desist from this sort of sporting.

The people of Tatao and the north-east islands are reported to have been in possession of books previous to the Chinese attack on Grand Lewchew, and to have been even more polished than in the principal island. Tatao and Ki-ki-ai are said to produce a sort of cedar, termed *kien-mou* by the Chinese, and *iseki* by the inhabitants, which is considered incorruptible, and brings a great price, the columns of the palaces of the grandees being generally formed of it.

The vessels of these islands, in the general appearance of their hulls and plan of rigging and sails, are precisely the same as we had observed throughout the whole of our track from the Gulf of Pe-che-lee to Napa-kiang. They had in common use, canoes hollowed from the trunk of a tree, much the same in shape as those of other parts of the world where they are employed, and of sufficient size to contain easily from six to eight or ten people. For purposes of heavier burden, they had boats strongly built, and rather flat-bottomed.

In these boats they brought our water, bullocks, and other stock, on board. The water was not sent in barrels, but in open tubs, and baled from these into our casks.

During our stay here, the Lyra was detached by the senior officer, in consequence of the people having told us that there was a closer and more secure harbour to the northward, to circumnavigate and examine the coast of the great island; which service Captain Hall performed, and returned to Napa-kiang, in seven days.

The state of cultivation was represented as very fine on a small island, which was named by captain Hall Sugar-loaf Island; and a town was observed, which had a very handsome appearance from the sea; trees, as usual, filling up the interstices between the houses, which rose from the water-side to the foot of the high land.

About twelve miles easterly from this island they anchored near an islet, which was named *Herbert's Isle;* and from thence proceeded in the boats to examine what seemed to be the mouth of a river; here it is reported there were not less than ten fathoms of depth within it, the whole passage being narrow, and the direction tortuous; in short they here discovered a harbour, not inferior in any respect, and in some superior, to Port Mahon, in

Minorca. The banks of this winding arm of the sea are high rocks, overgrown with climbing plants and flowers. It has, moreover, the advantage of Mahon of having a second outlet or communication with the sea: in short, it was discovered that an island in the mouth of a deep indent in the coast of the main island formed a circumnavigable passage, with safe anchorage in every part of it, and a sufficient depth of water for the largest class of ships, with good holding ground. It was named *Port Melville.*

In glens, formed by the opening of the rocks on its right bank, were observed several little villages, prettily situated; and the inhabitants were found to be the same civil creatures as on every other part of the island.

The north-eastern parts of the great Lewchew would appear not to be so populous, and therefore not so much cultivated, as the south-western side, or Cheouli, a greater extent of forest land being noticed; and on the western side also appeared to be the best and safest places for anchorages.

A few days previous to our leaving the island, intimation was sent that a man of the first distinction (said to be one of the princes, and nearest heir to the crown) intended paying a visit to the ship. He was carried down to the mouth of the little river, opposite to the anchorage, in a close chair, or palanquin, amidst an immense concourse of people, who had flocked from all parts to this spot.—He embarked in great state, in their own boats, with their flags flying; and was saluted, on his approach to the ships, by seven guns from each, and received on board the Alceste with every possible respect and attention; the rigging being manned, and the officers in full dress.—He was above the usual size of the Lewchews, and had rather more of an European countenance. His robe was of a dark pink-coloured silk; the cap rather lighter, with bright yellow flowers on it. In his mien and deportment there was much dignified simplicity; for, although his carriage was that of a man of high rank, it was totally unmixed with the least appearance of hauteur; and his demeanour was, altogether, extremely engaging.

As he passed along the decks, his own people saluted him by kneeling; clasping the hands before their breasts and bowing the head. He examined minutely every thing about the ship, and seemed equally pleased and surprised with all he saw. After joining in a sumptuous collation in the cabin, he took his leave with the same honours as when he came on board, having previously invited the captain and officers to an entertainment on shore. The day appointed for this feast happening to be the 25th of October, the anniversary of our venerable sovereign's accession to the throne, a royal salute was

N

fired, at sun-rise, by both ships; at noon the standard was hoisted, the ships dressed in colours, and another salute fired; after which the boats, with their flags flying, containing the captains and every officer that could possibly be spared, proceeded into Napa-kiang.

They were received precisely as on the former occasion, except that the number of grandees was greater, and there appeared a higher degree of state. The prince received the party at the gate, and conducted them into the hall. Three tables were laid close to each other; the first for the *great man* and the captains, the second for the superior officers, and the third for the young gentlemen. This prince, or chief, did the honours of his own table, occasionally directing his attention to the others; but a man of some rank was added to each of them, for the purpose of seeing the strangers properly treated, as well as to pass and proclaim the toasts; and for this purpose they were allowed to be seated, all the rest standing round the room, but, at the same time, joining heartily in the general mirth and glee. The healths of our king and royal family were toasted with much respect, and the anniversary of his majesty's accession was a day of real jubilee at Napafoo. The sovereign of Lewchew, the queen and princes, were proposed by our party; whilst they (never deficient in politeness) toasted the wives and children of their friends, the *Engelees*. In dining on board the ship, captain Maxwell had given confectionary to those who were married, in parcels, proportioned to the number of children they had; and on this occasion they returned the compliment; in the distribution of which, it was quite amusing to see some of the young midshipmen acquiring at once *wives and large families*.

Some personal presents from the captains were on this day offered to the chiefs, consisting of various articles as before, adding some damask table-cloths, and elegantly cut decanters and glasses, which they seemed highly to admire. Specimens of their manufactures in cloth were sent on board the ships in return.

At their departure, the prince attended the party nearly to the landing-place; and, when about to take his leave, two small additional presents (at the the suggestion of captain Hall) were given to him, as memorials. One was a very neat pocket thermometer (the use of the larger ones having been explained to him on board), and the other a cornelian seal set in gold, with a riband attached to each: they were hung round his neck; and the ceremony, being in public, had the appearance of investing him with an order, with which he seemed to be highly gratified. As the boats shoved off from the landing-place, the crews gave them three cheers, which they returned in their own style of salutation. They had sent on board the ship a great number of coloured paper lanterns, for the purpose of illuminating her at night, in honour of our king. This was done after dark, the lanterns being regularly ranged along the yards and rigging, the main-deck ports illuminated, sky rockets thrown up, and blue lights burnt at the yard arms, bowsprit, and spanker-boom ends, with a *feu-de-joie* of musketry, thrice repeated round the ship. The whole had a very brilliant effect from the shore, where thousands of the natives had collected to view the scene. About this time the boatswain's wife of the Alceste, who had been a good deal on shore, and was much noticed by the higher class of natives, had a splendid proposal made, by a deputation from some great man, to remain behind; a grand house to live in, and all manner of finery and attentions; great offers were also made to the boatswain to induce him to comply with this bargain; but (after two days' consideration) the negociation was broken off on the part of the husband, who refused to part with her. These proposals most likely came from the king, for it is not probable that any subject could have entered into a treaty of this sort.

A young lady of high rank, who had a great curiosity to see this *Inago-Engelese*, or Englishwoman, was brought to her one day when she was quite alone, and walked round her for a considerable time, eyeing her with great appearance of surprise.

The marriages of this country are not managed blindfold, as in China; but the young people are permitted to make their own choice, and to communicate without reserve. In China they would seem to have a superstitious dread of all foreign women; so much so, that any ship, having one or more on board, must land them at the Portuguese settlement of Macao, before they are permitted to pass up the river; as they fancy that their putting foot on the *celestial* soil would be attended with some great calamity to the country, or perhaps rather that their unrestrained liberty would be a bad example for their secluded females.

The rocks about the coasts of Lewchew were all of the coral kind; and immense masses, some assuming very odd shapes, were seen every where along the sea-shore; and some of the same formation were found on the higher land, and at some distance from the beach, whose situation is not easily to be accounted for, unless we suppose them to have been elevated by the force of volcanic fire.

The period of our departure being now fixed, all the stores were embarked on the evening of the 26th October. The next morning, as the ships unmoored, the Lewchews, as a mark of respect, arrayed themselves in their best apparel, and proceeding to the temple, offered up to their gods a solemn sacrifice, invoking them to protect *the Engelees*, to avert every danger, and restore them in safety to their native land! In the manner of this adieu there was an air of sublimity and benevolence combined, by far more touching to the heart than the most refined compliment of a more civilized people. It was the genuine benighity of artless nature, and of primitive innocence. Immediately following this solemnity, our particular friends crowded on board to *shake hands*, and say "Farewell!" whilst the tears which many of them shed, evinced the sincerity of their attachment. Even hard-faced Buonaparte was not unmoved; and, as the ships got under weigh, they lingered alongside in their canoes, displaying every sign of affectionate regard.

We stood out to seaward; and, the breeze being favourable, this happy island soon sunk from the view; but it will be long remembered by all the officers and men of the Alceste and Lyra; for, the kindness and hospitality of its inhabitants have fixed, upon every mind, a deep and lasting impression of gratitude and esteem.

Standing between what had been termed Lyra's Reef (where she had been so nearly lost) and the Southern Isles, we pursued our course to the south-westward. On the next day we saw Typinsan, one of the most considerable of the Lewchewan group;

and, on the 30th, descried Botel Tobago Xima, very much resembling, in its general features, St. Helena. Passing to the northward of it, we discovered, on the same day, the island of Formosa. The south-east part (that which we saw) is extremely high and mountainous, as, indeed, the whole of it is represented to be; and with the wind at N. E., as we then had it, and blowing strong, the surf rolled in with dreadful force upon the reefs extending from it*. Becoming too dark to see our way between the south end of the island, and the rocks of Vele Rete, we bore up, until, by our run, we

* The western parts of Formosa are under the dominion of the Chinese, but the eastern shores are still occupied by the aboriginal inhabitants. They are stated to be in a very uncivilized condition; that they can run with the swiftness of a greyhound: and are such expert marksmen with the bow and arrow, as to kill a pheasant on the wing with the greatest certainty. The water of the island is considered most insalubrious.

Their mode of courtship is rather odd: when a young man fixes his affections, he hovers about the house where the object of his regard resides, and plays upon some musical instrument, which signal she answers by coming out to meet him, and settle the matter, provided he is to her taste; should it be otherwise, she takes no notice, the gentleman *whistles in vain*, and must try his fortune elsewhere. The bridegrooms here transfer their filial duty to their fathers-in-law, and in fact are considered, after the marriage, as part of the wife's family.

were fairly to the southward of this danger, and then hauled to the wind on the starboard tack. The passage across the Straits of Formosa was boisterous in the extreme, blowing a severe gale at N. E., with that sort of tumbling sea felt in many other parts of the world, and which is infinitely more trying to ships than the long expansive swell of the wider ocean. The Alceste was a good deal injured, and the Lyra had nearly foundered, the fore-top sides giving way, and sustaining other damage. On the 2d November saw the grand Lemma; and on the same day pushed up to the anchorage, at the island of Lintin, without a pilot. Here we remained unnoticed for some days, when a number of men-of-war junks anchored near us, and a mandarin (their admiral) came on board, who, after the usual interrogatories, promised that a pass and pilot should be sent to us, to proceed up the river. In the time of Lord Anson, the Typa, near Macao, was of sufficient depth to receive the Centurion, a sixty-gun ship; but, at the present day, no frigate of large size can with propriety enter it, having become much shallower from the deposition of mud. To have brought up the provisions and stores for the use of the ships, which had been left at that place (subject to the conjoined impositions of the Chinese and Portuguese), in hired vessels, would have been expensive: the Lyra, therefore, was ordered down for that purpose.

We soon began to experience the inveterate ill-will of the viceroy, *Tsong-tou*, of Canton, who, well aware that the object of the embassy was in a great measure directed against his extortions, and those of his myrmidons, on our commerce, naturally entertained the most perfect hatred and detestation for any ship attached to such a mission. The people of Lintin (no doubt by the influence of their superiors) dammed up the course of the water; and it was not until sentries were placed along the little stream, to keep it clear, that we were enabled to fill our casks. The comprador, or the person employed to supply ships with provisions and necessaries, could only smuggle himself on board after dark; and then hurrying away trembling, for fear of being found near us at daylight with his boats. His master (or partner), *Aming*, had very lately been tortured, imprisoned, and fined; or, to use the Chinese phrase, *squeezed* in a very heavy sum, on suspicion that he knew of the intention of the captains of some Chinamen to proceed into the city, in order to present a memorial to the viceroy; and that he had not given information of this circumstance, that it might have been prevented. It seems the viceroy, in malicious feeling to the General Hewitt, because she had been connected with the embassy, would not permit her to load, under pretence that she was a *tribute ship*; that she must wait to carry back the unaccepted presents,

O

and of course *could have no room for teas.* Had it even been intended that she should carry back the presents (which was not the case, as, in the event of their not being received, they were to be otherwise disposed of), still they would not have occupied the tenth part of her tonnage; and, besides all this, it was no business of the viceroy to interfere with the arrangements about the *unaccepted tribute.* Captain Campbell, therefore, attended by a party of his brother officers, and some of the gentlemen of the factory, on finding other measures vain, proceeded to make a personal application to the viceroy, and to present a memorial, stating the great hardship and unreasonableness of this prohibition. This bold manœuvre, however, was unattended with success; and so far from the memorial being received, they were treated with every indignity, the people spitting in their faces. The General Hewitt was guarded with more rigour than ever, being surrounded by war junks; and, previous to our arrival, capt. Colin Campbell, of the navy, who, being unemployed, accompanied his brother in this voyage, with all who happened to be on board, were detained prisoners, at the second bar, for more than five weeks.

On the 11th another mandarin came on board, who disclaimed any knowledge of the former, or what he had promised, stating, through the medium of an interpreter (who seemed himself a man of some little consequence, and who evidently enjoyed peculiar satisfaction in repeating whatever was galling to the feelings of a Briton), that he had been *making fools of us* about sending a pass; that the embassador, had been sent away in disgrace from Pekin; that he must soon arrive here, when he would be immediately sent on board, and dismissed with all the English ships from the country, and so forth: adding that we must remain at our present anchorage, not attempting to pass up the river; and even, during our stay here, it would be necessary to have a security-merchant to answer for our good conduct. The latter part of this rhodomontade about a security-merchant for the king's ship, captain Maxwell begged might not be repeated, unless they wished to be thrown overboard; quietly telling them he would wait a reasonable time longer for the viceroy to send down a pass, or *chop*, to proceed up the river, which he was desirous of doing for two reasons: 1st, The ship required caulking and other repairs, which it was impossible to accomplish in her present unprotected and exposed situation. Next, the Lion, in the former embassy, had been admitted to a place of security; and the emperor having, in the first instance, expressed his pleasure that the Alceste should have the same reception, it could only be considered an indignity to be excluded; and would be *a bad precedent*. They now became a little more cool; and, after some desultory conversation, took their leave: but previously captain Maxwell insisted on their admitting (to exclude them from all shuffling), that, if a pass was not sent down in 48 hours, he was to take it for granted that leave was given.

That day arrived without the least notice being taken of us; and the pilot who had come on board, in the hope of carrying us up, sneaked off *in the dark*, saying it was dangerous for him to have any connexion with us.

Against an open attack a British commander can never be at a loss how to act; but the present was a most trying and embarrassing case, and imposed a very heavy and serious weight of responsibility. That his majesty's ship should be supplied by an *unauthorized* individual under cover of night, and by stealth, was not to be endured; to be denied admission to the harbour, and detained in an unprecedented manner, at this season of the year, in an open and dangerous road, could not be viewed but as an act of absolute hostility; and to all this were added sneering insult and contempt of the most mortifying kind.

To have waited longer for an explicit answer would have been vain; for a Chinese who could so far forget himself, even in the most common occasions of intercourse, as to give a frank, ingenuous, and *undesigning* reply to any communication, would be considered by his own countrymen a fool, and by foreigners a prodigy.

They are a people, who, by early education and constant habit, are *manœuvrers*, and always enjoy a much higher satisfaction in obtaining any purpose by fraud, trick, and overreaching, than by the most direct, candid, or honourable means; and afford a strong exemplification of the distinction between low cunning and true wisdom.

On the other hand, the king's representative was in their power, and this circumstance rendered a decision on the case still more difficult; but it was equally clear that the government which attempted to dishonour the flag would not respect the embassador; and experience has fully proved, that the tame submission of other nations has only added to the arrogance, and fostered the insolence of the Chinese. This, perhaps, was the impression on captain Maxwell's mind, when he got under weigh on the 12th; but not a word was expressed. The examination, however, of the locks and flints on the carronades by the gunner, with a few other minor preparations, were hailed as auspicious omens, and excited the most pleasing hopes; for the Chinese have no foreign friends; every seaman, whether of the navy or merchant's service, from experience of their faithless conduct, considering himself in a state of warfare from the moment he enters their territory. We got up as far as Lankeet Flat that night, without a pilot; but Mr. Mayne, the master, who knew the ground, volunteered to carry up the ship as far as she could go. Here we anchored for the night, and spoke the Cornwall Indiaman, bound homewards.

About two o'clock P. M. next day we again weighed, the flood tide serving, and beat up, towards the Bocca Tigris, or Bogue, then distant a few miles. The Bocca Tigris is the mouth of the principal branch of that river, on which Canton is situated, and where it is contracted to about the breadth of the Thames at London; but the banks are formed by high land, more especially on the east side.

The fortifications on this pass were formerly insignificant, and allowed to remain in a very dismantled state; but lately they have been repaired and strengthened with much care; an additional battery of forty guns being built, rather farther up, and on the same side with old Annan-hoy; a hundred and ten pieces of cannon, of different calibres, being at present mounted on these forts, including that of the island of Wang-tong opposite, the whole three being within half-gunshot of each other, with a garrison at this time of about 1,200 men.

Chumpee, which lies in a corner farther down, has about twelve or fourteen guns; but a ship *may* keep out of reach of them. As we advanced, some war-junks formed a line off Chumpee, and were soon after joined by several more, making altogether seventeen or eighteen. They carry, on an average, six guns, with from sixty to eighty men each. About this time (five o'clock) the same loquacious linguist before mentioned came on board from the mandarins, and desired, in a high and domineering tone, that the ship should be directly anchored, and that if we presumed to pass up the river, the batteries would instantly sink her; availing himself, at the same time, of that favourable opportunity, to express his personal *sense of low consideration* for us, and plainly telling the captain, he thought him very impertinent. The latter calmly observed that he would first pass the batteries, and then hang him at the yard-arm, for daring to bring on board a British man-of-war so impudent a message: his boat was then cut adrift, and himself taken into custody. The junks now commenced firing blank cartridge, which we returned with three guns from the ship, affecting to consider this as a mere salute. On the next tack we passed close to these warriors, who remained quiet until we got inside of them, and opened Chumpee; when that fort, little Annan-hoy, and the junks (now under weigh), began to fire with shot. At this moment the wind becoming light and baffling, we were obliged to drop anchor in Anson's bay, in order to hold the ground we had gained, and that they might not suppose they had driven us back; and in the act of wearing for this purpose, we gave the admiral of the junks a single shot only, by way of a hint*. They immediately ceased firing; and their junks anchoring near us, all remained quiet until a little after eight o'clock, when a light breeze sprung up, which enabled us to lay our course, and the anchor was again weighed. The moment this was observed by the junks, they beat their gongs, fired guns, and threw up sky-rockets, to give the alarm, and in an instant the batteries were completely illuminated, displaying lanterns as large as moderate-sized balloons, (the finest mark immaginable for us), commencing also a warm, but ill-directed, fire from both sides. Steering a steady course, the ship maintained a slow and regular fire, as the guns could be got to bear, without yawing her.

From the lightness of the breeze, which the cannonade seemed to lessen, it was a considerable time before we got abreast of the largest battery. At last, when within pistol-shot of the angle of it, and just before they could get all their guns to bear into the ship, a whole broadside, with cool aim, was poured in among them, the two-and-

* This first shot was fired by the captain's own hand, that in the event of the Chinese demanding those who fired, instead of those who ordered, or of seizing upon any innocent person, he might fully place himself in the situation of being individually responsible for all consequences.

thirty pounders rattling the stones about their ears in fine style, and giving them at the same time three *roaring* cheers.

This salvo was decisive at this particular point; their lights disappeared in a twinkling, and they were completely silenced; but from the island opposite they still continued their fire, the balls which passed over and around us striking New Annanhoy, which had thereby the full benefit of their own as well as our shot.

Soon after this our point was gained; and, standing up the river, we displayed our stern to these gentlemen. It is somewhat extraordinary that it should have been gained so easily; for, notwithstanding we were nearly an hour wrangling in this narrow passage, not a man (on our side) was killed, the ship only hulled twice, and some trifling damage done to the rigging. Almost any European gunners, with the same advantages, would have blown the frigate out of the water. During this affair, the flashing of the guns on the glassy surface of the river, and the rolling echo of their reports along the adjoining hills, had a very grand and animating effect. The Chinese linguist, who had crawled below when he saw matters taking a serious turn, and having observed there was no joking in the case, began in real earnest to think, as one part of the promise had been fulfilled, that *his* time had now arrived. Coming trembling upon

P

deck, he prostrated himself, and, kissing the captain's feet, begged for mercy. At that moment, hearing the order given to "stand by the larboard guns for Tiger Island" (on which we then supposed there was a battery), he said, with a rueful countenance, "What! no hab done yet?" "Not half done," was the reply: "How many guns have you got on Tiger Island?"—but, without waiting to answer this question, (or indeed reflecting in his perturbation that there were none at all), he wrung his hands, groaned heavily, and dived again below.

We stood on for some miles farther, and then anchored.—Next morning, before day, we found ourselves surrounded by their *grand fleet*; but they were wise enough to make no attack; for, having now broken the ice, it was too late for half-measures, and there was plenty of grape at hand to pick their teeth, had they offered the least molestation.

Half-measures seem to be a bad system in any dealings, but more especially with uncivilized people, for they are apt to attribute forbearance to fear, and acquire, under that impression, fresh courage.

When the late admiral Drury was induced to make a *show of force* at Canton, but was withheld, by circumstances, from proceeding to actual hostilities, there was no end to their gasconading; they considered his retiring as a great victory gained, and it is celebrated as such by an inscription in one of their pagodas.

On the morning of the 15th, the Alceste anchored among the Indiamen at second bar, still attended, but with perfect respect, by their fleet.

In the evening, captain Maxwell, attended by two gentlemen of the ship, proceeded in person to Canton to demand satisfaction (after having taken it) for the insult offered in firing upon the king's ship. On their way up they remained one evening with captain Campbell, of the Hewitt, and on that night, the news of the business with the batteries, having become public, much alarm was at first excited at Canton, as to the consequences of this measure; but the next morning they were agreeably surprised by the appearance of several tea-junks alongside, with part of her cargo, the viceroy having given permission for her *to load immediately!*—It also came to pass that the said viceroy thought proper to send down to the frigate, on this day, a high mandarin, attended by one of the Hong merchants, to wait upon the captain to welcome him into the river, and compliment him with all possible politeness!

It appeared, therefore, that the late *head-thumping* ceremony produced both tea and civility; and, most probably, it is the only mode of *Ko-towing**, by which we will ever receive either, on reasonable terms, from the Chinese. They affect, in their usual disingenuous cant, to despise our commerce; they say they could do perfectly well without it, and it is a mere matter of grace and favour that we are permitted to approach their shores, and carry on a trade highly to our advantage; but, when the company's agents were lately driven to the necessity of abandoning Canton, of stopping the trade, and giving up all concern with them, having actually taken their departure, struck the flag and flag-staff, and were on their way down the river, the Chinese authorities became alarmed, and sent after them to beg they would return, making such fair promises as patched up, for a time, their dif-

* *Ko-tow* is the ceremony exacted from all tributary princes and embassadors on approaching the presence of the emperor, and consists in kneeling, placing the hands forward, and then knocking the head thrice against the ground. *The patient* now stands upright, and, by word of command, kneels and knocks again, and afterwards a third time, making, in all, three prostrations, and *nine thumps*: and this is required not merely in the imperial presence, but on receiving any message, or donation of broken victuals, from the emperor, and was actually performed by the Dutch embassy for some half-gnawed bones in 1795. (Vide Van Braam's own account.) So that a man, to be much about court in China, would require a skull as thick as a buffalo's.

ferences. Neither will they trade honestly or say at once there is an end of all intercourse; and day after day we are insulted and trifled with by them.

The removal of our trade for a single year, and the appearance of a few of our lightest cruizers on their coasts, would throw the whole of this *celestial* empire into confusion; for they are not prepared for the loss that would occur in the one case, nor to meet the tumult and convulsion that would be excited by the destruction of their fisheries and coasting trade in the other. So feeble is their naval power, that, after warring with the pirates for many years, who chased their vessels up the river, and sacked the towns and villages within a few miles of Canton, they were at last obliged to compromise with them, bribing the whole to be quiet, and making their chiefs *first-chop* mandarins.

Krusenstern, the intelligent Russian navigator, who had occasion, in his voyage round the world, to touch at this port, where he experienced much vexation and insult, says, with great truth and propriety, what all equally feel, that "the forbearance and mistaken lenity of the greater civilized powers have emboldened these savages, not only to consider as barbarians all Europeans, but actually to treat them as such."

Captain Maxwell, on arriving at the city, sent in a strong note to the viceroy on the subject of his *rudeness* to the ship, which the latter answered by a letter *from the Hong merchants* to sir Theophilus Metcalfe, the chief of the factory, who told the merchants, that, having no control over the king's officers, he neither could receive nor communicate it. The Hong people next applied to captain Maxwell personally, with *their* letter of explanation about the *fracas* that had occurred; but he refused to receive them or their letter, on the ground that Chinese merchants were not the proper channel of communication between him and the viceroy. There the matter rested. The substance of this epistle was known to be some flimsy excuse about *a mistake* in sending down the chop or pass, which not being received by the mandarins at the forts, they were obliged to act according to orders. But what shewed the barefaced effrontery of their assertions was their public account of the business, whilst in the very act of presenting this letter of explanation (for they *affect* to give a public account of all transactions), which stated that the affair at the Bogue was a mere *chin-chinning* or saluting matter, altogether. The first report, previous to the official fabrication, was forty-seven killed, besides a number of men *spoiled** (wounded), which pro-

* Among these *wise and enlightened people*, if a man is materially *spoiled* he must die; for they neither will permit the necessary knowledge to be acquired for the performance of any operation, nor will they allow a stranger, who has

bably might be near the truth, considering they stood rather thick; but, after the appearance of the *edict*, it became a subject on which "*no man can talk**." This is what the Chinese call "*making face*," or keeping up appearances, with respect to any circumstances they are desirous of having reported their own way; and the people on the spot are literally ordered not to believe the evidence of their own senses; but to take the proclamation or edict† (as it is termed) for their guide, which is spread about in other parts, and handed down to posterity as good history, which no man dares to contradict. Few, it is supposed, will be credulous

that knowledge, to save him, but at the risk of his own life; as, in the event of the patient dying within forty days, from that or any other cause, the *anatomist* would certainly be strangled, or, if he had plenty of money, well *squeezed*, at least.

* There was, however, a good deal of talk, *sub rosa*, upon the subject, and the shot found in the battery having been sent up to Canton and weighed, they *hai-yawed* a great deal at what we termed our smaller ships, throwing shot of 25 *catties* (32lbs.) each, asking seriously about the probable consequences of the rejection of the embassy, and whether our larger ships could come up the river. The last accounts from China state that these feelings have rather increased than diminished.

† Some how or other the word edict has crept into general use for any piece of common information, whether it is from the emperor, or has the force of a law or not.

enough (who have ever been in China) to believe, that the people have the privilege of criticising the conduct of their superiors, and even of remarking publicly on the conduct of the emperor. *The law which permits them* to do so, may, indeed, be considered as a very severe piece of irony on their actual state.

That the viceroy had an intention of insult beyond the mere exclusion of the ship is rendered more than probable from the circumstance of a number of barges having been placed in the back passage to Macao, and not in the route of lord Macartney to Canton, which were removed from that situation immediately after the late occurrence; and likewise from the general tenour of his conduct throughout. Be this as it may, it would clearly have been a triumph to his cause, and that of his adherents, that the embassador should have arrived at Canton with as little eclat and appearance of respect as possible; it would have added (as exterior is every thing with them) in the eyes of the Chinese, as well as foreigners, to the idea of disgrace and discomfiture to an obnoxious mission. But the advance of the ship to Wampoa not only commanded as brilliant an entry for the embassy* as

* That the Chinese did not join in it, is only an additional proof that they would have prevented it, had they dared.

ever had been witnessed on any other occasion; but, what was of equal importance, it sustained the dignity of the flag, and reduced the viceroy (after offering every insult) to the meanness of congratulating those who had defied his flotilla and battered his fortifications.

Canton may be considered the most interesting city in China. It is one of the first in point of size, and, perhaps, the very first with respect to wealth; and here, as the native manners may be seen *in all their purity* as perfectly as in any other part, the traveller has also the advantage of viewing them as connected with Europeans, and of noticing their brightest efforts of *imitative* genius, which the encouragement afforded by the commerce of the place calls forth.

The numerous junks and boats of all descriptions in motion upon the Tigris surpasses even the busy scene displayed upon the Thames; for here the boats are the only residence of some thousand families, who live entirely on the water, and manage to obtain a livelihood, some by plying passage, others by fishing and picking up floating articles, and not unfreqently by exercising their talents like our *mud-larkers* and river pirates.

The appearance of the river at night, completely illuminated by the lamps and lanterns in all the boats, has a very pretty effect. Infanticide is said not to be so common in China as was at one time

Q

believed; but that it actually exists is not attempted to be denied even by the Chinese themselves; one of whom, on being interrogated seriously on this subject, readily admitted, without seeming to consider it as a crime, that they certainly did drown their children when they were so numerous as to be inconvenient to them; but that boys might be exposed alive, and, if picked up, they became coolees or slaves. It would appear, therefore, that female children are most likely to become the victims in this way, from being less useful to their parents when they grow up; for the patriarchal law of China considers the sons as slaves of their father; and he is entitled to sell them as such, should occasion require. The entertainments given by the Hong merchants at Canton to their European friends are considered to be very superb. Seldom fewer than a hundred people sit down in the great hall to dinner, which is usually dressed in our style (although they have also their *chop-stick* feasts), and plenty of the best viands, wines, and fruits, cover the table. Bird-nest soup is also handed round as a great treat, to which the Chinese attribute very extraordinary and invigorating qualities. On us, however, it produced no unusual effect; and we should not have known it from any other, had it not been pointed out. These bird-nests, which are collected in the Sunda Archipelago, are rather expensive articles, being purchased by an equal weight of silver.

Their composition is not yet exactly known, but it is some gelatinous substance, most likely of the vegetable kind, which the swallow's pick up.

During the whole of the entertainment, a play is performing on a stage erected at one end of the hall the subject of which it is difficult, in general, for an European to comprehend, even could he attend to it for the deafening noise of their music. By collecting together in a small space a dozen bulls, the same number of jack-asses, a gang of tinkers round a copper caldron, some cleavers and marrow-bones, with about thirty cats; then letting the whole commence bellowing, braying, hammering, and caterwauling together, and some idea may be formed of the melody of a Chinese orchestra*. Their jugglers are extremely adroit, and the tumblers perform uncommon feats of activity.

The Chinese government, with regard to religion, is tolerant. It appears to be in *wordly* concerns only that it is tyrannical, and seems to be indifferent as to what a man professes, provided he does not interfere in state affairs. Some one, calling himself a catholic bishop, was, a short time before our arrival, strangled in one of the provinces, being

* Their softer music, employed at their weddings, and other occasions unconnected with the stage, is not unpleasing to the ear.

suspected of intermeddling with temporal matters, and promoting the late rebellions. Another was said to be under sentence of death on the same accusation.

They not only worship their own tutelary deities, but they are represented as making offerings to evil spirits, or, as it is vulgarly termed in this country, they "hold a candle to the devil," in order to avert mischief. They have not the advantage of any particular day set aside for public worship, nor do they attend their temples congregationally. Their priests or bonzes are not treated with that reverence and respect which is justly and reasonably due to the *respectable* ministers of religion in all countries. They are otherwise free, however, from indecorum and irregularity, having no wild fanatics, such as exist in India; they are not troubled with domineering *spiritual* inquisitors, as in some of our neighbouring countries; nor have they any impious quacks and mountebank preachers, abusing toleration and dishonouring religion, as in England.

The Chinese are strangers to love: from the spirit of their institutions, which unnaturally prohibit all intercourse between the sexes, that passion can never be felt; and marriage is a mere cold-hearted bargain, conducted through the medium of some female agent, whenever a man finds it convenient to have a wife. As he never sees the lady until he unlocks the door of the sedan chair in which she is brought home, the key of which is previously sent to him, he is of course very liable to have tricks played upon him.—For example, more especially as polygamy is allowed, a man may have a wife sufficiently young to be considered his daughter; should he want money, and the lady another husband (both very likely cases), or from any other reason should they wish to part, and think proper to act in collusion, she is sold as his daughter to another man, who is thus imposed upon by having a second-hand wife palmed off upon him, instead of a new one. The rigour of the law against offenders of this kind, which awards a very severe bambooing to all principals, aiders, and abettors, affords a proof that frauds of this description are not unfrequent.

With a people who still imagine the earth to be a plane, and China in the middle, with all her tributary kingdoms around her; who are equally uninformed with regard to astronomy; who, in the prohibition of the study of the human frame, preclude the attainment of the very basis of all medical knowledge; and who, in fact, in every branch of natural philosophy, are equally ignorant, and resolved to continue so; it is evidently impossible to connect the term *science* in any shape or manner.

The natural productions of the country, and their acquaintance with agriculture and the arts (as far as they have been able to advance for that glorious edict which stamped them perfect, and commanded they should not proceed beyond the bounds of excellence), have already been (and probably may be again, with additional information) described, by those whose peculiar opportunities, as well as talent for observation, enable them to speak fully, and with precision, on those subjects.

The government of China, however plausible it may sound in theory, is, by all that can be observed in a transient view, and, by every concurrent testimony of residents in the country, most iniquitous and tyrannical in practice. The mandarins, and even the emperor, it is true, cannot boldly and openly chop off heads like a Turkish bashaw or the dey of Algiers: but they have the knack of rendering life very miserable, and assume the power of bambooing, torturing, fining *(or squeezing)*, and every species of oppression short of death. The human kind can scarcely be more degraded than in China, for no where is power more diabolically perverted. Their laws, with the exception of some absurdities (such, for example, of visiting mere accidental homicide with the same punishment as the most deliberate murder), *read very well;* and, were they duly and impartially administered, might be found sufficiently adapted (as all laws ought to be) to the genius and character of the people they are formed for; but this is by no means the case; bribery and corruption being so common, as scarcely to be the objects of indignation or remark.

A few years since an affray took place (as usual) between some of the seamen of the Indiamen who were at Canton on leave, and the Chinese mob, in which one of the latter by an unlucky blow was killed. The Chinese authorities demanded blood for blood, one of the seamen having been seized and detained in the factory: this, however, was not tamely yielded to (as in the case of the innocent gunner, who was sacrificed in so cowardly a manner many years ago), but was resisted on the ground either of the aggression of the Chinese, or of a mutual inclination to fight, in which a man happened to be killed, without the least previous intention of murder. Fortunately the Lion, of 64 guns, captain Rolles, happened to be there, which probably gave some weight to these arguments; and the mandarins, having no objections to compromise the matter for money, proposed that a certain sum should be paid to them for *the benefit of the deceased's relations*, and a slave could then be purchased of the Portuguese at Macao, who might be strangled in lieu of one of the sailors, and thus *the law would be perfectly satisfied!*

It may easily be imagined this proposal was not acceded to; and, at last, after much discussion, the matter was arranged in some way or other without resorting to this horrible mode of expiation*.

It is lamentable to observe that the institutions of any nation should have the effect of deadening every feeling of sympathy, and of exciting, instead of discouraging, "man's inhumanity to man;" but such is the case in this country; and when any one is severely wounded by accident, or falls into a river, or other situation of danger, he is certain of receiving no assistance from the by-standers, who will most probably take to their heels, in order to *save themselves* from being the last person seen near him.

About midnight, some time in November, 1816, when the Alceste was lying at second bar, the shrieks of some people in the water were heard near the ship. The hon. Mr. Stopford, who had the watch, and another gentleman, collecting a few individuals who happened to be on deck, jumped into a boat alongside; pushed off to their assistance; and, directed by their cries, picked up, one after the other, three Chinese, who were plunging about in the river, which is here several miles wide.

* Related by J. Cotton, Esq., of the English factory at Canton.

It was a fine night, and a number of small junks were moving up under easy sail, several of whom passed within a few fathoms of these people who were bawling for help; and although they could, without the slightest difficulty, have saved the whole, they continued their course, the crews standing upon deck, and viewing their struggles with the most callous indifference.

On carrying the three men on board the frigate, it appeared they had been crossing the river at this place, in a little *Sanpan*, or boat; in which were, besides themselves, the wife and child of one of them; and that this boat had been run down by one of the headmost junks, which passed on without taking the least notice, and regardless of their fate, although they had occasioned the mischief; the others coolly following their example; when they were fortunately heard from the ship, and preserved by the boat. The poor woman and child, being unable to swim, sank, and were drowned.

Before day-light these people got a passage on shore by a boat which happened to be passing near the ship, and in the course of the forenoon one of them returned on board with a *cumshaw*, or present, of three wild ducks, which he presented on his knees to the gentleman who had saved him, stating that, by the junk running over their sanpan, he had lost his wife and a bull child (his only mode of expressing a boy), and must himself with the

R

other men have perished also but for the assistance we afforded them. Pleased with this appearance of heart and gratitude, where so little was expected, some money and provisions were given him for his ducks, and he was allowed to bring on board fish, and other articles for sale, which, from becoming rather a favourite, soon enabled him to repair the loss of his boat.

The Chinese, viewing them in every point, are assuredly a very singular race, and afford a melancholy example of the perverseness of human nature; exhibiting a people who have had for some thousand years a dawn of civilization, which, from the operation of the most narrow-minded principles, has never brightened into day. But for the presumptuous folly of supposing themselves at the summit of perfection, and the absurd tyranny of fettering the human understanding, by forbidding all innovation and improvement, China might and ought to have been at the present hour the greatest nation of the world. Instead of impotent and gasconading pretensions to universal supremacy, she might have enjoyed, from her early and local advantages, the real glory of being the seat of arts, literature, wealth, and power.

What have the governors or the governed gained by this *pretended* non-intercourse, and stupid contempt of the rest of mankind? The frequent change of dynasty and constant rebellions tend to show that the former have been by no means secure; whilst the debased and humiliated state of the people sufficiently evinces that their sordid and illiberal plan confers no benefit on the general mass.

The Chinese, however, are not without their admirers. Some attribute their suspicious meanness, knavery, silly pride, and other ill qualities, to their depraved mode of government, which narrows their ideas, by compelling their attention, and attaching importance, entirely to the observance of useless forms and ceremonies; and by admitting of no deviation from one contracted path, even in the simplest transactions of life; and that, were it not for these shackles of the mind, they would be a gay, civil, industrious, and honest people. Perhaps there may be a good deal of truth in this argument, and it is, therefore, extremely unfortunate that some change does not take place in a system which produces effects so injurious to the reputation of mankind. Another, and very distinct class of encomiasts (of the true antediluvian school), affect to hold them in high estimation, solely on account of their unvarying habits, and tenacious adherence to their ancient customs; and as they are now, in all respects, precisely what they were two or three thousand years ago, they venerate them as living monuments of former times, and as *valuable specimens of the antique*. In their present state, however, from whatever cause it is produced, few moderns will take their leave of them with sentiments of regard or estimation; and even the most inveterate antiquarian, had he more concerns with them than those merely speculative, might be divested, perhaps, of some of his prejudices.

Of the embassy, we had heard nothing distinctly for nearly five months, except that it had not been received; and it was not clearly understood until its arrival at Canton, that the refusal to submit to a humiliating ceremonial, considered as stamping it with a character purely tributary, was the cause of this failure; and that a reception on the unconditional terms of the Chinese would have been deeemed more prejudicial to the objects of the mission than even a rejection by firm resistance. But these weighty matters are foreign to the subject of a mere simple sea-voyager, and will be so well described by those officially connected with them, as to render any farther observation unnecessary. Although the viceroy of Canton was in daily communication with the legate, or commissioner, appointed to accompany the embassy through the country, yet he maintained a sullen silence as to the probable period of its arrival, making no communication that we might prepare for that event; and it was not until the 31st of December that a letter of old date, having been detained for some time, was put into captain Maxwell's hand, from lord Amherst, stating when the embassy was likely to enter Canton, which took place on the following day. A procession of boats, consisting of the barges of the two men of war, those of the factory, the American consul, and all the Indiamen, who were very numerous, with their respective flags, the captains and officers in full dress, and the boats' crew in uniform clothing, proceeded some miles up the river, where they fell in with the Chinese barges, having the embassy on board. This meeting was highly gratifying to both parties, after a separation of nearly five months, during which each had, in its respective route, observed many novel scenes, and encountered extraordinary occurences.

Lord Amherst removing into his own (or the Alceste's) barge, a double line of boats was formed on each side, and in this order proceeded down the river, and was landed at the entrance of the great temple, on the Honan side, from whence he was conducted to his residence by a very numerous assemblage, who had collected to receive him. The apartments in this place had been fitted up with much taste, and great appearance of comfort, under the inspection of Mr. Urmston, of the factory, and was by far the most commodious and respectable quarters they had met with in China. A temporary building, or wooden frame covered with yellow screens, and containing a chair of state, having also yellow ornaments and the usual insignia of the emperor, was erected in the principal square, for the occasion of the viceroy's interview with the embassador, in order to deliver the emperor's letter to the prince regent. This ceremony took place some days after the arrival of his lordship. The viceroy had been ordered by his court to make a speech to the embassador, on presenting this letter (which speech had been in rehearsal for some months, and the subject of it publicly known through the medium of Portuguese translations); and it appeared that the tenour of this embryo harangue was rather of an insulting nature, containing such expressions as "Your good fortune has been small;" "You sighed after happiness, and were unable to lift your eyes up to heaven," *i. e.* to view the celestial emperor, and others of a similar kind. The preamble of this edict also stated, that there appearing to be no want of respect in the king or prince, who had sent over so many seas to pay him homage, but that the fault lay in the embassador's not understanding the rules of true politeness; he therefore had accepted some trifling articles of the presents of the said king, and in return had bestowed precious gifts, agreeably to the maxim of Confucius, "Take little, and give much;" and that, "on the receipt of these gifts, the embassadors became exceeding glad, and expressed great contrition * for their conduct;" and went on to say "that the viceroy, on their arrival, was to give them an entertainment in compliance with good manners, after which he was to rid himself of them as soon as possible; and should they again *supplicate* him to accept their presents, he was enjoined to say to them, "The edict has passed and cannot be revoked! the emperor can be troubled no more!" and so forth. As it appeared this intended address had been made by them matter of public notoriety, it was understood, that, in order to prevent any *palaver* of this sort, a hint was given to the viceroy the day previous to the interview, cautioning him against the use of any improper language, as it might call forth replies which would be unpleasant. At the time appointed this meeting of ceremony took place, and was accompanied by the appearance of guards, music, and other attendants, there being much state observed on each side.

* A tolerably strong example of this sort of *face-making* occurred during the discussion about the performance of the ceremony, in which the precedent of lord Macartney's not having done it was brought forward, when the emperor declared, through his ministers, that he himself had seen his lordship perform it; and they coolly called on Sir G. Staunton, who had been page in that embassy, to vouch for the truth of the fact.—That he did submit to the Ko-tow is no doubt the *face* they have put upon it in all the records of the empire.

The emperor's letter contained in a bamboo case, covered with yellow silk, was now taken from this throne, and presented to the embassador, who transferred it to his secretary; and the persons on either side, who were (by previous regulation) allowed chairs, having taken their seats, and the usual unvarying number of complimentary questions having been gone through, such as "What age are ye?" and some others of the same high importance, the viceroy began to state, through the medium of Mr. Morrison, who interpreted, "By the favour of the emperor you have traded to this country for more than a hundred years, very much to your advantage." "Tell him," said lord Amherst, "the advantage is mutual." This being done, the viceroy replied, "No, the advantage is very much on your side." "Repeat to him," said his lordship, "that the advantage is *strictly* mutual." From the dignified and independent manner in which this was spoken (a manner which, of course, from his peculiar situation, and the different style of those he had to deal with, he could have no conception of), and perceiving, also, a determination to repulse every thing bordering on impertinence, he seemed to be quite awed and disconcerted; the thread of his discourse was broken, and he got no farther on with this mighty specimen of altiloquence, than to say something about "the subject being a disagreeable one;"

when the embassador considering the public business ended by the presentation of the emperor's letter rose up, and, wishing him a very good morning, retired in the same state as on coming to this hall of audience.

On the 20th, every thing being ready, his excellency left Canton on the forenoon of the 20th January, 1817, and was attended to Wampoa in the same style as on entering it, except that, in passing the various ships in that branch of the river, each saluted with nineteen guns, the Chinese war-junks also saluting. It appeared that the viceroy, just as the embassador had embarked in his barge to proceed down the river, approached near in his boat, and made a tender of a complimentary card, which was not accepted, it being deemed an improper time and mode of presenting it. On the 21st the Alceste weighed and stood down the river; and, on the morning of the 22d, as we passed our friends at the forts, each battery fired a distinct salute, in honour of the embassador, as did the different war-junks; and their whole military force, exclusive of that in the batteries, was drawn out in line in Anson's Bay, and fired a *feu-de-joie* with their matchlocks.

The ship answered all these in rotation, with three guns to each. On the same evening we anchored off the city of Maçao, and the next morn-

S

ing his excellency landed; but here the ghost of the late queen made its way through the centre of the earth, (for we were now antipodes to the Brazils), and prevented any public attentions being paid to the embassador, because the accounts of her death had just arrived. The fact is, these poor people dare not, were they ever so willing, do any thing which they think may be displeasing to the Chinese, under whom they live in a state of miserable thraldom; the latter having it in their power, and frequently resorting to the measure, of stopping their allowance of provisions whenever they display the least symptom of being unruly; and in the present case it seemed to be the wish of the Chinese to have the whole management of the honours to the embassador; a mandarin receiving him on going on shore, although within their walls, precisely as he would have done, had the Chinese flag, instead of that of the Portuguese, been flying there.

Macao is stated to be a possession of little or no value to the crown of Portugal, and, under the circumstances of its present tenure, certainly not one that is either honourable or independent. The cave of Camoens is the only object here which attracts the notice of a traveller, from its being the spot in which he composed his celebrated poem of the Lusiad. Camoens, certainly the greatest, and perhaps the only, Portuguese poet whose fame ever extended beyond the boundaries of his own country, deserved a better fate; and it is painful to think he died a beggar in the streets of Lisbon.

On the 9th January, the embassador having re-embarked, we took our leave of China, steering for Manilla, the capital of the Philippines, or Spanish India, where we arrived on Monday the 3d of February, but found it was only Sunday at this place, owing to the different routes by which the Spaniards and the Portuguese advanced to the Asiatic seas; the one by Cape Horn, the other by the Cape of Good Hope; a circumstance which may produce an awkward effect on people newly arrived at Manilla;—for instance, a stranger invited to a party on Wednesday, without at all reflecting on the way he came thither, might dress himself for the occasion, and make his appearance on Tuesday. The town of Manilla, from its peninsular situation, having on one side the sea, and on the other a deep and rapid river, with strongly-fortified ditches across the isthmus, ought to be, with a proper garrison, very defensible, for there are no commanding heights in its immediate vicinity; but their soldiers consist almost entirely of mulattoes and blacks, and seem to be in a very lethargic state of discipline.

The Metees, or Mulatto women, who are a mixture between the Spaniards and the natives, are remarkable for their symmetry of form and stately mien, and this sort of beauty is so universal as hardly to admit of an exception. The religion of the Indians under the immediate controul of the Spaniards is Christianity; but at Mindanao and the other islands (of which there are more than a thousand), where they are governed by their own sultans, it is said to be a mixture of Mahomedanism with their original Pagan rites. The banks of the river, as well as the lake from which it issues, called the Laguna de Bria (its nearest part about eighteen miles from the city), are represented as extremely beautiful, and abounding in tropical scenery.

This lake extends more than thirty miles into the interior. Near its head are some remarkable hot springs, called "Los Baños," or baths; but they seemed rather too hot for that purpose. Luconia* is about four hundred miles in length, and two hundred in breadth; and, were it made

* Canada is said to have derived its name from the Spaniards, when they landed in that quarter, repeating the words "aca nada," or "nothing here" (meaning there was no gold to be found), which the Indians caught the sound of. Some similar occurrence appears to have occasioned the name of Luçon. When Magellan's party first went on shore they found one of the native women beating rice, as is usual at the present time, in a mortar hollowed from the trunk of a tree, and, finding herself surrounded by strange men, she held up to them the large wooden pestle, calling

the most of, is fully capable of affording all the productions of either Western India or of the neighbouring Archipelago.

It is so healthy, that the medical people have scarcely any practice, and complain that there are no "enfermedades reynantes," or reigning diseases, such as the yellow fever, as it exists at the Havannah, Vera Cruz, Carthagena, and other settlements more (by their reckoning) to the eastward. This misfortune most probably proceeds from the very limited intercourse which Manilla has, compared to any of the others, with Europeans, or *new-comers*, the Spaniards who inhabit it being almost without exception creoles*, and therefore assimilated, from their birth, to the climate. This restricted intercourse may be observed in there not being a single inn for the accommodation of strangers in the whole city of Manilla or its suburbs. Chinese emigrants are here in thousands, and are very industrious and money-making, being the chief artificers and traffickers in small matters, resembling the lower class of Jews. From their being found scattered about in all the Indian islands,

out Looson, which is the native term for it; and this becoming a bye-word among the Spaniards, they named the island Luçon, which has been modernized into Luconia.

* This term does not mean a person having the least mixture of black blood, but merely a white born in the country.

they might indeed be considered as the Jews of the east, were they only half as honest.

The Spaniards appear not to be fully in possession of Luconia at the present day. They may be said, indeed, only to be masters of the ground they occupy in a military point of view, for, by their own accounts, it is not only dangerous to travel without an escort in the country, but it is not safe for a Spaniard to walk out singly after dark about the suburbs of Manilla. A day or two after our arrival, three of the natives, who had been concerned in the murder of a marchioness, were strangled before the porch of one of their churches. These people seemed to have been actuated not by a spirit of plunder, but of revenge, for some real or supposed injuries, as the deed was committed in the public square, by dragging her from the carriage on her return home in the evening; and in this way frequent assassinations occur. A gentleman of the Alceste being in a party one evening, where observations on the murderous character of the natives were the subject of conversation, took occasion to observe that if such was the case it would be necessary to keep a look-out in going homewards; but he was assured that, as an English officer, he had nothing to fear. "No, Señor, temen ustedes, pero matan a nosotros," "They are afraid of you, but they kill us." It cannot be fear alone that induces the natives to spare the English officers, who certainly freely exposed themselves at times and in situations the most favourable for assassination, without suffering the slightest injury; and it is probable that a French, German, or any other transitory stranger might do the same; for it evidently is to their own immediate rulers that this feeling of hostility exists; and it is no doubt the result of their impolitic mode of governing. Such a state of things would render the Philippines a very easy conquest to any invading force in time of war; but the court of Spain, at present, seems to have most to fear from those sentiments of independence which have extended from Buenos Ayres to Manilla, and appear to be a point of union in which almost all classes are agreed, not excepting even the hierarchy.

The celebrated and unfortunate Pérouse, when at this place in his voyage of discovery, made the following remarks:—"Manilla is built on the shore of a bay of the same name, which is more than twenty-five leagues in circumference. It lies at the mouth of a river, navigable as far as the lake from which it rises, and is, perhaps, the most delightfully situated city in the world. Provisions of all kinds are in the greatest abundance there, and extremely cheap; but clothing, European hardware, and furniture, bear an excessively high price. The want of competition, together with the prohibitions and restraints of every kind laid on commerce, render all the productions of India and of China at least as dear there as in Europe; and this colony, although the various imports bring near 800,000 piastres annually into the treasury, costs Spain 1,500,000 besides, which are sent there every year from Mexico.

"The immense possessions of the Spaniards in America have not admitted of the government essentially directing its attention to the Philippines, which resemble the estates of those great lords whose lands lie uncultivated, though capable of making the fortunes of many families. I should not hesitate to assert, that a very great nation possessed of no other colony than the Philippine Islands, and who should establish the best government of which they are capable, might behold all the European settlements in Africa and America without envy.

"Three millions of inhabitants people these various islands, of whom that of Luconia contains nearly one-third. These people appear in no respect inferior to those of Europe. They cultivate the earth like men of understanding; are carpenters, joiners, smiths, goldsmiths, weavers, masons, &c. I have walked through their villages, and found them kind, hospitable, and communicative; and, though the Spaniards speak of and treat them with contempt, I perceived that the vices they attributed to the Indians ought rather to be imputed to the government they have themselves established." Speaking of no encouragement being given to labour, he states that "as soon as the inhabitants have the quantity of rice, of sugar, and of vegetables, necessary for their subsistence, the superflux is of no value whatever. In such circumstances, sugar has been sold for less than a halfpenny the pound, and the rice remained upon the ground without being reaped.

"It would be difficult for the most unenlightened society to form a system of government more absurd than that which has regulated these colonies for the last two centuries.

"The port of Manilla, which ought to be free and open to all nations, has been till very lately shut against Europeans, and open only to a few Moors, Americans, and the Portuguese of Goa. The governor is invested with the most despotic authority; and the audiencia, which ought to moderate his power, is totally impotent before the representative of the Spanish government. In point of fact, though not by law, it lies in his breast to admit or confiscate the merchandise of foreigners whom the hope of advantage may have brought to Manilla, and who would not expose themselves to this risk but on the probability of a very great profit, ultimately ruinous to the consumers." It is undoubtedly as unaccountable, as it appears to be unenlightened, that a nation should

T

take deliberate measures to make a colony a burden to it, which is not only fully able to maintain itself, if permitted, but to enrich the mother country. It seems almost equal to that of restoring the inquisition.

The Spanish authorities here were marked in their attentions to the embassador during his stay; and, on the 9th of February, having re-embarked, we got under weigh, bound homeward, and parted company with our consort, the Lyra, who proceeded from hence with dispatches for India.

A course was now shaped to avoid the numerous rocks and shoals not well defined, which lie in that part of the Chinese Sea more immediately to the westward of the Philippines, and to the north-westward of Borneo; and having by the 14th passed the whole, and got into the usual track for the passage of either the Straits of Banca or Gaspar, it was resolved to proceed through the latter, as being more direct and less subject to calms than the former, and considering them equally safe from the latest surveys and directions being on board, some of them by those who had personally examined them. At day-light in the morning of the 18th we made Gaspar Island exactly at the time expected, and, passing it, stood on for the Straits. As is customary in approaching any coast or passage whatever, but more especially one that all are not familiarly acquainted with, the utmost precaution was taken by keeping the leads going in both chains, men looking out at the mast-heads, yard-arms, and bowsprit-end, the captain, master, and officer of the watch, on whom the charge of the ship at such a time more particularly devolves, having been vigilantly on deck during the whole of the previous night and this morning. Steering under all these guarded circumstances, the soundings exactly corresponding with the charts, and following the express line prescribed by all concurring directions to clear every danger (and the last danger of this sort between us and England), the ship about half-past seven in the morning struck with a horrid crash on a reef of sunken rocks, and remained immovable!

It was very soon indeed but too evident that any attempt to move her would be attended with the most fatal consequences; for, on each side of the rocks on which she hung, the water deepened from ten to seventeen fathoms immediately around her; and, from the injury received, she must have gone down in a few minutes, had she forced her way over this narrow reef. The best bower anchor was therefore let go, to keep her fast; and the pumps were soon abandoned, being clearly of no avail.

The boats were now hoisted out, and lieutenant Hoppner, with the barge and cutter, ordered to proceed with the embassador and suite, and all those not essentially required, to the nearest part of the island, which seemed about three miles and a half distant. Meanwhile every exertion was used by the captain and officers, who remained by the ship, to secure what provisions and stores could be obtained; a task of considerable labour and difficulty, for all was under water, which now rose above the orlop-deck.

When she struck the tide must have been rising, for towards the afternoon it fell outside, and consequently inside the ship several feet, thereby enabling us to save ourselves from absolute starvation by laying hold of some articles of provender which floated up, assisted by divers, and which the boats were employed in conveying to the shore. A raft was also constructed, on which were placed the heavier stores, with some baggage, and towed towards the island. By the return of those boats which carried his excellency on shore we learnt the very great difficulty of effecting a landing, the mangrove-trees growing out to a considerable distance in the water; and it was not until after ranging along-shore for nearly three miles from the place they first attempted that a small opening appeared, through which, by scrambling from rock to rock, they at last obtained a footing on *terra firma*. Here, by cutting away a quantity of the smaller jungle at the foot of a hill (for the island was completely overgrown with wood), a space was cleared away, where, under the shade of the loftier trees, they bivouacqued for that day and night.

On board the ship the work went on with activity, endeavouring to save whatever might be most useful on such an occasion; but, as the tide rose, the swell of the sea lifting her from the rocks, she dashed on them again with such violence, as to render it necessary about midnight to cut away the topmast. At day-light on Wednesday the 19th, Mr. M'Leod landed with two men who had been severely wounded by the fall of the masts, and with a report from the captain to lord Amherst. The spot in which our party were situated was *sufficiently romantic*, but seemed at the same time the abode of ruin and of havoc. Few of its inhabitants (and among the rest the embassador) had more than a shirt or pair of trowsers on. The wreck of books, or, as it was not unaptly termed, "a literary manure," was spread about in all directions; whilst parlimentary robes, court-dresses, and mandarin habits, intermixed with check shirts and tarry jackets, were hung around in wild confusion on every tree.

On his lordship being informed that no fresh water had as yet been obtained from the ship, and that it was barely probable some might be got by scuttling the lower deck, he desired every body might be called around him, and ordered that a gill of that which had been sent on shore the day before (what happened to be on deck in the drip-stones and water-jugs), with half that quantity of rum, should be equally served out to every man without distinction, and, taking his own share with perfect good humour, afforded to others an example of calm fortitude, and a cheerful readiness to share in every privation, which never fails on such occasions to have a powerful and beneficial effect, more especially when that example is found, where it ought to be, in the first rank.

Parties were now returning who had been searching for water in vain, every attempt to dig for it having proved fruitless, or being too near the sea, salt water alone had oozed into the pits. At one spot they found the skeleton of a man, and the horrid idea of his having died from thirst rushed on every mind. Those who went into the wood, on these excursions, were obliged to notch the trees, and leave marks as they advanced, in order to find their way back. In the forenoon captain Maxwell came on shore, to confer with lord Amherst on the best mode to be adopted in the perilous situation they were then placed. The boats were utterly incapable of conveying half our number any where; and, as some must necessarily go to the nearest friendly port for assistance, captain Maxwell judged it best that his excellency and suite should proceed with a proper guard for Batavia, or whatever part of Java they could fetch, from whence vessels could be despatched to bring off those who remained behind.

This being what is termed the north-west monsoon, there was every likelihood of the boats reaching Java (the current being also in their favour) in three days; and by this arrangement, which very happily was settled without loss of time, two grand purposes were answered, the nearest to the captain's heart, and his duty, viz., the immediate conveyance of the embassador and suite to a place of safety; and, by their safety, ensuring more effectually than by any other means that of the officers and men who remained with himself upon this desert isle. It was thought probable that row-boats might be despatched from Batàvia after the arrival of his excellency, so as to reach the island (even against wind and current) in twelve or fifteen days; and as Mr. Ellis volunteered to return with the first boat or vessel that shoved off to our assistance, an additional assurance was thus given, that, combined with the influence of the embassador with the Dutch government, no delay would occur in forwarding relief. After a short, and very slender *fête champêtre* in this wilderness (in which salt was viewed with the same horror as arsenic), his lordship about five in the evening, accompanied by the gentlemen of his suite, by lieutenant Hoppner, in command of the boats, Mr. Mayne to navigate, lieutenant Cooke, R. M. (with a party as officers of the guard, in the event of falling in with any of the Malay pirates who infest these seas), Mr. Blair, midshipman, and Mr. Somerset (who had come to see the world a little), waded out to the edge of the reef, and embarked in the barge and cutter. They were in all forty-seven persons, and had with them a small stock of provisions, consisting of a side of mutton, a ham, a tongue, about twenty pounds of coarse biscuit, and some few more of fine, seven gallons of water, the same of beer, as many of spruce, and about thirty bottles of wine. This was all that could be spared; and being deemed equal to sustain nature for four or five days, in which period they must either make the land, or be so disposed of as to require no provisions, it was considered sufficient. After pulling outwards a little way to clear all the rocks, they made sail to the southward, attended by the best wishes of every man of the island, and were soon out of sight. The number left behind was 200 men and boys, and one woman.

The first measure of captain Maxwell, after fixing a party to dig a well in a spot which was judged, from a combination of circumstances, the most likely to find water, was to remove our bivouac to the top of the hill, where we could breathe a cooler and purer air; a place in all respects not only better adapted to the preservation of our health, but to our defence in case of attack. A path was cut upwards, and a party employed in clearing away and setting fire to the underwood on the summit. This last operation tended much to free us from myriads of ants, and of snakes, scorpions, centipedes, and other reptiles, which in such a place and climate generally abound. Others were employed in removing upwards our small stock of provisions, which were deposited (under a strict guard), in a sort of natural magazine, formed by the tumbling together of some huge masses of rock on the highest part of this eminence. On board the wreck a party was stationed, endeavouring to gain any accession they could to our stock of provisions and arms, and to save any public stores that could be found. There was a communication for this purpose between the shore and the ship whenever the tide permitted. For the last two days every one had experienced much misery from thirst: a small cask of water (the only one which could be obtained from the ship) was scarcely equal to a pint each in the course of that period; and perhaps no question was ever so anxiously repeated, as "What hope from the well?" About eleven at night the diggers had got, by rather a tortuous direction (on account of large stones), as far down as twenty feet, when they came to a clayey or marly soil, that above being a red earth, which seemed rather moist, and had nothing saline in the taste. At a little past midnight a bottle of muddy

U

water was brought to the captain as a specimen, and, the moment it was understood to be fresh, the rush to the well was such as to impede the workmen; and it was necessary to plant sentries to enable them to complete their task, and permit the water to settle a little. Fortunately about this time a heavy shower of rain fell, and, by spreading sheets, table-cloths, &c., and wringing them, some relief was afforded. There are few situations in which men exposed without shelter to a torrent of rain would, as in the present instance, hail that circumstance as a blessing: bathing in the sea was also resorted to by many in order *to drink by absorption*, and they fancied it afforded relief.

Thursday, 20th. This morning the captain, ordering all hands together, stated to them in few words, that every man, by the regulations of the navy, was as liable to answer for his conduct on the present as on any other occasion; that, as long as he lived, the same discipline should be exerted, and, if necessary, with greater rigour than aboard, a discipline for the general welfare, which he trusted every sensible man of the party must see the necessity of maintaining; assuring them, at the same time, he would have much pleasure in recommending those who distinguished themselves by the regularity and propriety of their conduct; that the provisions we had been able to save should be served out, although necessarily with a very sparing hand, yet with the most rigid equality to all ranks, until we obtained that relief which he trusted would soon follow the arrival of lord Amherst at Java. During this day the well afforded a pint of water for each man; it had a sweetish milk-and-water taste, something like the juice of the cocoa-nut, but nobody found fault with it*; on the contrary, it diffused that sort of happiness which only they can feel who have felt the horrible sensation of thirst under a vertical sun, subject at the same time to a harassing and fatiguing duty. This day was employed in getting up every thing from the foot of the hill; boats passing to the ship, but unfortunately almost every thing of real value to us in our present case was under water. We were in hopes, however, that, as no bad weather was likely to happen, we might be enabled, by scuttling it at low water, or by burning her upper-works, many useful articles might be acquired.

On Friday (21st), the party stationed at the ship found themselves, soon after day-light, surrounded by a number of Malay proas, apparently well armed, and full of men. Without a single sword or musquet for defence, they had just time to throw themselves into the boat alongside, and push for the

* It was *happily said*, when mixed with a little rum, to resemble milk punch; and we endeavoured to persuade ourselves that it was so.

shore, chased by the pirates, who, finding two of our other boats push out to their assistance, returned to the ship, and took possession of her. Soon afterwards it was reported, from the look-out rock, that the savages, armed with spears, were landing at a point about two miles off. Under all the depressing circumstances attending shipwreck; of hunger, thirst, and fatigue; and menaced by a ruthless foe; it was glorious to see the British spirit staunch and unsubdued. When the order was given for every man to arm himself in the best way he could, it was obeyed with the utmost promptitude and alacrity. Rude pike-staves, were formed by cutting down young trees; small swords, dirks, knives, chisels, and even large spike-nails sharpened, were firmly affixed to the ends of these poles; and those who could find nothing better, hardened the end of the wood in the fire, and, bringing it to a sharp point, formed a tolerable weapon. There were, perhaps, a dozen cutlasses; the marines had about thirty muskets and bayonets, but could muster no more than seventy-five ball-cartridges among the whole party. We had fortunately preserved some loose powder drawn from the guns on the upper deck after the ship had struck, (for the magazine was under water in five minutes), and the marines by hammering their buttons round, and by pieces of broken bottles rolled up in cartridges, did their best to supply themselves with a sort of langrage which would have some effect at close quarters, and strict orders were given not to throw away a single shot until sure of their aim. Mr. Cheffy, the carpenter, and his crew, under the direction of the captain, were busied in forming a sort of abattis by felling trees, and enclosing in a circular shape the ground we occupied; and, by interweaving loose branches with the stakes driven in among these, a breast-work was constructed, which afforded us some cover, and must naturally impede the progress of any enemy unsupplied with artillery. That part of the island we had landed on was a narrow ridge, not above musket shot across, bounded on one side by the sea, and on the other by a creek, extending upwards of a mile inland, and nearly communicating with the sea at its head. Our hill was the the outer point of this tongue, and its shape might be very well represented by an inverted punch-bowl: the circle on which the bowl stands would then shew the fortification; and the space within it our citadel.

It appeared by the reports of scouts, a short time after the first account, that the Malays had not actually landed, but had taken possession of some rocks near this point, on which they deposited a quantity of plunder brought from the ship; and during the day they continued making these predatory trips.

In the evening all hands were mustered under arms, and a motley group they presented; it was gratifying, however, to observe, that, rude as were their implements of defence, there seemed to be no want of spirit to use them if occasion offered*. The officers and men were now marshalled regularly into the different divisions and companies, their various posts assigned, and other arrangements made. An officer and party were ordered to take charge of the boats for the night, and they were hauled closer into the landing-place. An alarm which occurred during the night shewed the benefit of these regulations, for, on a sentry challenging a noise among the bushes, every one was at his post in an instant, and without the least confusion.

On Saturday morning (22d), some of the Malay boats approached the place where ours were moored; and, with the view of ascertaining whether

* Even the little boys had managed to make fast a table-fork, or something of that kind, on the end of a stick, for their defence. One of the men who had been so severely bruised by the falling of the masts, and was slung in his hammock between two trees, had been observed carefully *fishing*, or fixing, with two sticks and a rope-yarn, the blade of an old razor.---On being asked what he meant to do with it, he replied, "You know I cannot stand; but, if any of these fellows come within reach of my hammock, I'll mark them."

they had any inclination to communicate on friendly terms, the gig, with an officer and four hands, pulled greatly towards them, waving the bough of a tree (a general symbol of peace every where), shewing the usual demonstration of friendship, and of a desire to speak to them; but all was vain, for they were merely reconnoitering our position, and immediately pulled back to their rock.

The second lieutenant (Mr. Hay) was now ordered with the barge, cutter, and gig, armed in the best way we could, to proceed to the ship, and regain possession of her, by fair means, or by force; the pirates not appearing, at this time, to have more than eighty men. Those on the rocks, seeing our boats approach, threw all their plunder into their vessels, and made off.

Two of their largest proas were now at work on the ship; but, on observing their comrades abandon the rock, and the advance of the boats, they also made sail away, having previously set fire to the ship, which they did so effectually, that in a few minutes the flames burst from every port, and she was soon enveloped in a cloud of smoke. The boats were unable to board her, and therefore returned.

Here was a period to every hope of accommodation with these people, if, indeed, any reasonable hope could ever have been entertained on that head. The Malays, more especially those wandering and piratical tribes, who roam about the coasts of Borneo, Billiton, and the wilder parts of Sumatra, are a race of savages perhaps the most merciless and inhuman to be found in any part of the world. The Battas are literally cannibals. In setting fire to the ship, they gave a decided proof of their disposition to us; but, although certainly with no good intention, they did merely what we intended to do; for, by burning her upper works and decks, every thing bouyant could float up from below, and be more easily laid hold of.

The ship continued burning during the whole of the night; and the flames, which could be seen through the openings of the trees, shed a melancholy glare around, and excited the most mournful ideas. This night also all hands were suddenly under arms again, from a marine firing his musket at what he very properly considered a suspicious character near his post, who appeared advancing upon him, and refused to answer after being repeatedly hailed. It turned out afterwards that the branch of a tree, half cut through the day before, had given way, under one of a race of large baboons, who, we found about this time, disputed the possession of the island with us. At the well, where there generally was kept a good fire at night, on account of the mosquitoes, the sentries had more than once been alarmed by these gentlemen shewing their black faces from behind the trees.

They became extremely troublesome to some ducks we had saved from the wreck, (carrying them up the trees with them, and letting them fall down again when alarmed), which, on several occasions, left their little yard, and came up among the people, when the monkeys got among them, instinctively preferring the society of man for protection.

On Sunday morning (23d), the boats were sent to the still-smoking wreck, and some flour, a few cases of wine, and a cask of beer, had floated up. This last God-send was announced just at the conclusion of divine service, which was this morning held in the mess-tent, and a pint was ordered to be immediately served out to each man, which called forth three cheers*. This seems to be the only style in which a British seaman can give vent to the warmer feelings of his heart. It is his mode of thanksgiving for benefits received; and it equally serves him to honour his friend, to defy his enemy, or to proclaim victory. This day we continued improving our fence, and clearing

* Some *decorously righteous* man observing to the chaplain that he had never seen such a scene in England as the congregation cheering at the church-door; the latter replied, with proper liberality (and tolerable good humour), "perhaps you never saw a thirsty English audience dismissed with the promise of a pint of beer a piece."

X

away a glacis immediately around it, that we might see and have fair play with these barbarians, should they approach. They had retired behind a little islet (called Pulo Chalacca, or *Misfortune's Isle*), about two miles from us, and seemed waiting there for reinforcements; for some of their party had made sail towards Billiton.

Monday morning (24th), the boats, as yesterday, went to the wreck, and returned with some casks of flour only partially damaged: a few cases of wine, and about forty boarding-pikes, with eighteen muskets, were also laid hold of. With the loose powder secured out of the great guns in the first instance, Mr. Holman, the gunner, had been actively employed, forming musket cartridges; and by melting down some pewter basins and jugs, with a small quantity of lead, lately obtained from the wreck, balls were cast in clay moulds, increasing not a little our confidence and security. A quart of water each had been our daily allowance from the well hitherto, and on this day a second was completed near the foot of the hill, in another direction, which not only supplied clearer water, but in greater plenty; and we could now, without restriction, indulge in the luxury of *a long drink*, not caring even to excite thirst, in order to enjoy that luxury in higher perfection.

On Tuesday (25th), the boats made their usual trip; some more cases of wine and a few boarding-pikes were obtained, both excellent articles in their way, in the hands of men who are inclined to entertain either "their friends or their foes." On shore employed completing the paths to the wells, and felling trees which intercepted our view of the sea.

Wednesday (26th), at day-light, two of the pirate proas, with each a canoe astern, were discovered close in with the cove where our boats were moored. Lieutenant Hay, (a straight-forward sort of fellow), who had the guard that night at the boats, and of course slept in them, immediately dashed at them with the barge, cutter, and gig. On perceiving this, they cut adrift their canoes, and made all sail; they rather distanced the cutter and gig, but the barge gained upon them. On closing, the Malays evinced every sign of defiance, placing themselves in the most threatening attitudes, and firing their swivels at the barge. This was returned by Mr. Hay with the only musket in the boat, and, as they closed nearer, the Malays commenced throwing their javelins and darts, several falling into the barge, but without wounding any of the men. Soon after they were grappled by our fellows, when three of them having been shot, and a fourth knocked down with the but-end of the musket, five more jumped overboard and drowned themselves (evidently disdaining quarter), and two were taken prisoners, one of whom was severely wounded.

They had taken some measure to sink their proa, for she went down almost immediately. Nothing could exceed the desperate ferocity of these people. One who had been shot through the body, but who was not quite dead, on being removed into the barge, with a view of saving him (as his own vessel was sinking), furiously grasped a cutlass which came within his reach, and it was not without a struggle, wrenched from his hand: he died in a few minutes. The consort of this proa, firing a parting shot, bore up round the north end of the island, and escaped. Their canoes were also brought on shore, containing several articles of plunder from the ship. They appeared to be the two identical proas which set fire to her. The prisoners (the one rather elderly, the other young) when brought on shore, seemed to have no hope of being permitted to live, and sullenly awaited their fate; but, on the wounds of the younger being dressed, the hands of the other untied, and food offered to them, with other marks of kindness, they became more cheerful, and appeared especially gratified, seeing one of their dead companions, who had been brought on shore, was decently buried.

The Malays are a people of very unprepossessing aspect; their bodies of a deep bronze colour; their black teeth and reddened lips (from chewing the betel-nut and siri), their gaping nostrils, and lank clotted hair hanging about their shoulders and over their scowling countenances, give them altogether a fiend-like and murderous look. They are likewise an unjoyous race, and seldom smile.

The state of one of the wounds received by the Malay (his knee-joint being penetrated, and the bones much injured) would have justified, more particularly in this kind of field practice, amputation; but, on consideration that it would be impossible to convince him of this being done with the intention of benefiting him, and might have the appearance of torture, which it was not improbable might suggest the idea of amputation and other operations to them, in the event of any, or all of us, falling into their hands, it was determined, therefore, to try the effect of a good constitution, and careful attention. A little shed was built, and a blanket and other comforts given to him, and his comrade appointed his cook and attendant. They refused at first the provisions we offered them; but, on giving them some rice to prepare in their own way, they seemed satisfied. Never expecting quarter, when overpowered in their piratical attempts, and having been generally tortured when taken alive, may account for the others drowning themselves.

In the forenoon, immediately after this *rencontre*, fourteen proas and smaller boats appeared standing across from the Banca side, and soon after they anchored behind Pulo Calacca. Several of their people landed, and carrying up some bundles on their shoulders, left them in the wood, and returned for more. We had some hope, from the direction in which they first appeared, as well as their anchoring at that spot (the rendezvous agreed upon at the departure of lord Amherst), that they might have been from Batavia to our relief.

The small flag (belonging to the embassy) was brought down and displayed on the look-out rock; the strangers, each, immediately hoisted some flag at their mast-head. Anxious to know still more about them, Mr. Sykes was allowed to advance with the union jack, accompanied by some more of the young gentlemen, along the strand to a considerable distance; and soon after some of their party, with a flag, set off to meet them. As they mutually approached, the Malays dropped a little in the rear of their flag-bearer, and laid down their arms; ours also fell astern, and the two ancients (or colour men), wading into a creek which separated them, cautiously met each other. The Malay *salamed* a good deal: many fine Yorkshire bows were made on the other side: shaking hands was the next ceremony, and then, joining flags, they walked up arm and arm to the place where the captain and several others were stationed. Satisfied now they must be friends sent to our assistance, they were welcomed with cheers, and every countenance was gladdened. But our joy was of short duration; for, although their flag was laid submissively at the captain's feet, and all was sufficiently civil in their deportment, yet they turned out to be mere wanderers, employed gathering a sort of sea-weed, found on the coast of these (but in still greater abundance among the Pelew) islands, said by some to be an article of commerce with the Chinese epicures, who use it like the bird-nests in their soups. All this was made out chiefly by signs, added to a few Malay words which some understood.

Mr. Hay, with his division armed, proceeded down to their anchorage himself, and some other officers, going on board with their rajah (as they styled him), who expressed a great desire to see the captain on board, and sent him a present of a piece of fish, and some cocoa-nut milk. During the night many schemes were proposed as to the best mode of negotiating with these people. Some thought that, by the hope of reward, they might be induced to carry part of us to Java, and our four remaining boats would then be equal to the conveyance of the rest. Others, adverting to the treacherous character of the Malays, and the great temptation to murder us when in their power, from that sort of property still in our possession, and *to them* of great value, considered it safest to seize upon and disarm them, carrying ourselves to Batavia, and then most amply to remunerate them for any inconvenience they might have sustained from being pressed into the service.

The morning of Thursday, the 27th, however, perfectly relieved us from any further discussion on this subject, the rajah and his suite having proceeded to plunder the wreck, which by this time they had espied. It is probable they were not certain of our real situation on the first evening, but might have supposed, from seeing the uniforms, colours, and other military appearance, that some settlement, as at Minto, had been established there; and this may also account for their civility in the first instance, for, from the moment their harpy-like spirit was excited by the wreck, and they saw our real condition, there were no more offerings of fish, or of cocoa-nut milk.

To have sent the boats openly to attack them was judged impolitic; it would only have driven them off for a moment, and put them on their guard against surprise by night, should it be thought necessary, in a day or two, to do so. They could deprive us of little; for the copper bolts and iron work, which they were now most interested about, were not to us of material importance.

We had the day before moved the boats into another cove, more out of sight (from the overspreading branches of the trees), and safer in case of attack, being commanded by two strong little ports (one having a rude draw-bridge), erected on the rocks immediately above it, and wattled in, where an officer and piquet were nightly placed; and a new serpentine path was cut down to this inlet, communicating with our main position aloft.

On Friday, the 28th, the Malays were still employed on the wreck. A boat approached us in the forenoon; but on the gig going out to meet it, they refused to correspond, and return to their party. No relief having appeared from Batavia, and the period being elapsed at which (as was now thought) we had reason to expect it, measures were taken, by repairing the launch, and constructing a firm raft, to give us additional powers of transporting ourselves from our present abode, before our stock of provisions were entirely exhausted.

On Saturday, the 1st of March, the Malays acquired a great accession of strength, by the arrival of fourteen more proas from the northward (probably of the old party), who joined in breaking up the remains of the wreck.

At day-light, on Sunday, the 2d, still greater force having joined them during the night, the pirates (leaving a number at work on the wreck) advanced with upwards of twenty of their heaviest vessels, towards our landing-place; fired one of their patereroes; beat their gongs; and, making a hideous yelling noise, they anchored in a line, about a cable's length from our cove. We were instantly under arms, the party covering the boats strengthened, and scouts sent out to watch their motions, as some of their boats had gone up the creek, at the back of our position; and to beat about, lest any should be lying in ambush from the land. About this time, the old Malay prisoner, who was under charge of the sentries at the well, and who had been incautiously trusted by them to cut some wood for the fire, hearing the howling of his countrymen, left his wounded comrade to shift for himself, ran off into the wood, and escaped, carrying with him his hatchet. Finding, after waiting a short time in this state of preparation, that they made no attempt to land, an officer was sent a little outside the cove in a canoe, waving in a friendly manner, to try how they would act. After some deliberation, one of their boats, with several men armed with creeses, or their crooked daggers, approached: here, as usual, little could be made out, except a display of their marauding spirit, by taking a fancy to the shirt and trowsers of one of the young gentlemen in the canoe; but, on his refusing to give them up, they used no force.

A letter was now written, and addressed to the chief authority at Minto, a small settlement on the north-west point of Banca, stating the situation in which we were placed, and requesting him to forward, if in his power, one or two small vessels to us, with a little bread and salt provisions, and some ammunition. Again the officer went out in the canoe, and was again met by the Malay boat. This letter was given to them, the word Minto repeatedly pronounced (which they seemed to understand), the direction pointed out, and signs made that on their return with an answer they should be rewarded with abundance of dollars, shewing them one as a specimen. This was done more to try them than with any hope of their performing the service; for, although a boat went down to Pulo Chalacca (where they appeared to have somebody in superior authority), yet none took the direction of Banca. Meantime their force rapidly increased, their proas and boats of different sizes amounting to fifty. The larger had from sixteen to twenty men; the smaller about seven or eight; so that, averaging even at the lowest ten each, they had fully five hundred men. The wreck seemed now nearly exhausted, and appeared to be a very secondary object, knowing the chief booty must be in our possession, and they blockaded us with increased rigour, drawing closer into the cove, more especially at high water, fearful lest our boats, being afloat at that period, should push out and escape them. In the afternoon some of the rajah's people (whom we at first considered our friends) made their appearance, as if seeking a parley; and, on communicating with them, gave us to understand by signs, and as many words as could be made out, that all the Malays, *except their party*, were extremely hostile to us; that it was their determination to attack us that night; and urging also that some of their people should sleep up the hill, in order to protect us. Their former conduct and present connexions displayed so evidently the treachery of this offer, that it is needless to say it was rejected, giving them to understand *we could trust to ourselves*. They immediately returned to their gang, who certainly assumed a most menacing attitude. In the evening, when the officers and men were assembled as usual under arms, in order to inspect them, and settle the watches for the night, the captain spoke to them with much animation, almost verbatim as follows: " My lads, you must all have observed this day, as well as myself, the great increase of the enemy's force, for enemies we must now consider them; and the threatening posture they have assumed. I have, on various grounds, strong reason to believe they will attack us this night. I do not wish to conceal our real state, because I think there is not a man here who is afraid to face any sort of danger. We are now strongly fenced in, and our position in all respects so good, that, armed as we are, we ought to make a formidable defence against even regular troops: what then would be thought of us, if we allowed ourselves to be surprized by a set of naked savages, with their spears and creeses? It is true they have swivels in their boats, but they cannot act here. I have not observed that they have any matchlocks or muskets; but, if they have, so have we. I do not wish to deceive you as to the means of resistance in our power. When we were first thrown together on shore, we were almost defenceless; seventy-five ball-cartridges only could be mustered: we have now sixteen hundred! They cannot, I believe, send up more than five hundred men; but, with two hundred such as now stand around me, I do not fear a thousand, nay, fifteen hundred of them! I have the fullest confidence we shall beat them; the pike-men standing firm, we can give them such a volley of musquetry as they will be little prepared for: and, when we find they are thrown into confusion, we'll sally out among them, chase them into the water, and ten to one but we secure their vessels. Let every man therefore be on the alert with his arms in his hands; and, should these barbarians this night attempt our hill, I trust we shall convince them that they are dealing with Britons." Perhaps three jollier hurras were never given than at the conclusion of this short but well-timed address. The woods fairly echoed again; whilst the picquet at the cove, and those stationed at the wells, the instant it caught their ear, instinctively joined their sympathetic cheers to the general chorus.

There was something like unity and concord in such a sound, (one neither resembling the feeble shout nor savage yell), which, rung in the ears of these gentlemen, no doubt had its effect; for about this time (8 P. M.) they were observed making signals with lights to some of their tribe behind the islet. If ever seamen or marines had a strong inducement to fight, it was on the present occasion, for every thing conduced to animate them. The feeling excited by a savage, cruel, and inhospitable aggression on the part of the Malays,—an aggression adding calamity to misfortune,—roused every mind to a spirit of just revenge; and the appeal now made to them, on the score of national character, was not likely to let that feeling cool. After a slender but cheerful repast, the men lay down as usual upon their arms, whilst the captain remained with those on guard to superintend his arrangements. An alarm during the night shewed the effect of preparation on the people's minds, for all like lightning were at their posts, and returned growling and disappointed because the alarm was false.

Day-light on Monday the 3d, discovered the pirates exactly in the same position in front of us; ten more vessels having joined them during the night, making their number now at least six hundred men.

"The plot began to thicken," and our situation became hourly more critical. Their force rapidly accumulating, and our little stock of provisions daily shortening, rendered some desperate measure immediately necessary.

That which seemed most feasible was by a sudden night attack, by our four boats well armed, to carry by boarding some of their vessels, and, by manning them, repeat our attack with increased force, taking more, or dispersing them. The possession of some of their proas, in addition to our own boats (taking into consideration that our numbers would be thinned on the occasion), might enable us to shove off for Java, in defiance of them. Any attempt to move on a raft, with their vessels playing round it, armed with swivels, was evidently impossible. Awful as our situation now was, and every hour becoming more so; starvation staring us in the face, on one hand, and without a hope of mercy from the savages on the other; yet were there no symptoms of depression, or gloomy despair; every mind seemed buoyant; and, if any estimate of the general feeling could be collected from countenances, from the manner and expressions of all, there appeared to be formed in every breast a calm determination to dash at them, and be successful; or to fall, as became men, in the attempt to be free.

About noon on this day, whilst schemes and proposals were flying about, as to the mode of executing the measures in view, Mr. Johnstone (ever on the alert), who had mounted the look-out tree, one of the loftiest on the summit of our hill, descried a sail at a great distance to the southward, which he thought larger than a Malay vessel. The buz of conversation was in a moment hushed, and every eye fixed anxiously on the tree for the next report, a signal-man and telescope being instantly sent up. She was now lost sight of, from a dark squall overspreading that part of the horizon, but in about twenty minutes she again emerged from the cloud, and was decidedly announced to be a square-rigged vessel. "Are you quite sure of that?" was eagerly inquired:—"Quite certain," was the reply:—"it is either a ship or a brig standing towards the island, under all sail!—The joy this happy sight infused, and the gratitude of every heart at this prospect of deliverance, may be more easily conceived than described. It occasioned a sudden transition of the mind from one train of thinking to another, as if waking from a disagreeable dream. We displayed our colours on the highest branch of the tree, to attract attention, lest she should only be a passing stranger.

The pirates soon after this discovered the ship (a signal having been made with a gun by those anchored behind Pulo Chalacca), which occasioned an evident stir among them. As the water was ebbing fast, it was thought possible, by an unexpected rush out to the edge of the reef, to get some of them under fire, and secure them. They seemed, however, to have suspected our purpose; for, the moment the seamen and marines appeared from under the mangroves, the nearest proa let fly her swivel among a party of the officers, who had been previously wading outwards*, and the whole, instantly getting under weigh, made sail off, fired at by our people, but unfortunately without effect; for, in addition to the dexterous management of their boats, the wind enabled them to weather the rocks. It was fortunate, however, this circumstance took place, and that it had the effect of driving them away; for, had they stood their ground, we were as much in their power as ever, the ship being obliged to anchor eight miles to leeward of the island, and eleven or twelve from our position, on account of the wind and current; and, as this wind and current continued the same for some time afterwards, they might, most easily (with their force), have cut off all communication between us. Indeed it was a most providential and extraordinary circumstance, during this monsoon, that the ship was able to fetch so far up as she did. *The*

* The shot was picked up by one of the young gentlemen, and appeared to be of malleable iron, not quite round.

Z

blockade being now raised, the gig, with Messrs. Sykes and Abbot, was despatched to the ship, which proved to be the Ternate, one of the company's cruizers, sent by lord Amherst to our assistance, having on board Messrs. Ellis and Hoppner, who embarked the day of their arrival at Batavia, and pushed back to the island.

The gig was able to return (being a light boat); but our friends, who attempted to pull ashore in the cutter, were compelled to put back, after struggling with the current for nine hours, during the night of Monday, and morning of Tuesday, the 4th. That day was employed in getting all the moveables we had saved from the wreck ready for embarkation. Wednesday, the 5th, landed Messrs. Ellis and Hoppner:—the recollection of the voluntary promise made by the former at parting, now fulfilled, and re-appearing as a deliverer, added to the many interesting and peculiar circumstances of the meeting, gave a new glow to every feeling of friendship, and, on entering Fort Maxwell, they were received with heartfelt acclamation by the whole garrison, under arms.

This fortification and its inhabitants had altogether a very singular and romantic look. The wigwams (or dens, as they were called) of some, neatly formed by branches, and thatched with the palm-leaf, scattered about at the feet of the majestic trees, which shaded our circle; the rude tents of others;

the *wrecked*, unshaven, ragged appearance of the men, with pikes and cutlasses in their hands, gave, more especially by fire-light at night, a wild and picturesque effect to this spot, far beyond any robber scene the imagination can portray.

Two of the Ternate's boats also arrived with a twelve-pounder carronade, some round and grape, and musket ammunition, in the event of the pirates thinking proper to return before we had finished our business; which, from the difficulty of communicating, required the whole of Wednesday to perform.

On Thursday, the 6th, the majority of the officers and men embarked in the boats (now increased in number), and proceeded to the Ternate; the raft, also, with four officers and forty-six men (and a cow), got under sail, and, after a comfortable cold-bath navigation, reached the ship after dark. Every article which could not be carried off, and was thought might be of the slightest use to the savages, was piled into a heap, on the top of the hill, and made into a bonefire.

At midnight the boats returned to bring off captain Maxwell, and those remaining with him; the whole arriving safe on board on the morning of the 7th March. We were most hospitably received by captain Davidson and his officers*.

* The wounded Malay was also carried to Batavia; and he is now (although with rather a disabled joint) most probably employed on board the Ternate.

The island of Pulo Leat is about six miles long, and five broad; situated about two degrees and a half to the southward of the equator: it lies next to Banca, and is in the line of islands between it and Borneo. It is uninhabited, and, as far as we could explore (and exploring was no easy task), produces nothing for the use of man. We found a great number of the rinds of what we afterwards discovered at Batavia to be the far-famed and delicious mangustin, which only thrives near the line;—the baboons, who manage to live here, having monopolized all the fruit. Had we found any entire, we might have indulged in them, even without knowing their nature; as, more especially in a case of short commons, like ours, there could be no great danger in following the example of a monkey.

The soil of the island would appear to be capable of affording any production of the torrid zone, and, if cleared and cultivated, would be a very pretty place: the tree which produces the caoutchouc or indian rubber grows here.

The small stock of provisions saved from the wreck, and the uncertainty of our stay there, rendered economy in their distribution, as well as the preventing any waste or abuse, a most important duty. The mode adopted by captain Maxwell, to make things go as far as possible, was to chop up the allowance for the day into small pieces, whether fowls, salt beef, pork, or flour, mixing the whole hotch-potch, boiling them together, and serving out a measure of this to each, publicly and openly*, and without any distinction. By these means no nourishment was lost; it could be more equally divided than by any other way; and, although necessarily, a scanty, it was not an unsavoury, mess. All the bread, except a few pounds, was lost. The men had half allowance of rum divided between dinner and supper (sometimes more on hard fags), and the officers two glasses of wine at dinner, and a quarter allowance of rum (a small dram-glass) at supper.

A small bag of oatmeal was found one morning, which some of the young Scotch midshipmen considered as *their own*, and sat down, with great glee, round a wash-hand basin* full of *burgoo*, made from it; but they reckoned too securely on the antipathies of their English friends, for (not thinking this, perhaps, a proper time for indulging national prejudices) they claimed their share, and managed to get through it without a wry face.

* Truth requires it to be stated, and it may naturally be supposed, that, among so many, one or two progging sort of people might be observed, who had no disinclination to a little more than their just allowance; but the general feeling was much too manly and fine to admit of contamination.

* Not the only extraordinary mess-dish which this occasion had reduced some to.

The guards at the posts, covering the boats, were generally under charge, alternately, of Messrs. Hay, Casey, Johnstone, Sykes, Abbot, Brownrigg, and Hope. The *garrison duty*, at night, was conducted, in turns, by the surgeon, chaplain, Messrs. Eden, Raper, Mostyn, Stopford, and Gore; thus making it light, and enabling them to keep their eyes open, and walk vigilantly round to observe that all the sentries were on the alert, and called out every quarter of an hour; the younger midshipmen being perched, in rotation, on the look-out rock during the day, to watch the motions of the pirates, and give notice of any ship or vessel which might appear in the offing.

It is somewhat remarkable, that, during our stay here of nineteen days, exposed alternately to heavy rains, and the fierce heat of a vertical sun, none were taken sick, and those who landed so (some very ill), all recovered, except a marine, who was in the last stage of a liver complaint, contracted whilst in China, as one of the guard to the embassador. Another man, of very troublesome character, thought proper to leave his companions on the third day after landing. He may have been bit by a serpent in the woods, and died there, or have fallen into the hands of the savages; but he was never afterwards heard of. We marked with oil and blacking, in large characters, on the rocks, the date of our departure, to be a guide to any that might come there in quest of us, and in the afternoon of the 7th, we bid adieu to Pulo Leat, where it is not wonderful that, in our situation, we should have suffered some hardship and privation; but it is remarkable, indeed, that, surrounded by so many dangers, the occurrence of any one of which might have proved fatal, we should have escaped the whole. We had, for example, great reason to be thankful that the ship did not fall from the rocks on which she first struck into deeper water, for then all must have perished;—that no accident happened to the boats which conveyed the embassy to Batavia; for, in that case, we should never have been heard of;—that we found water;—that no mutiny or division took place among ourselves;—that we had been able to stand our ground against the pirates;—and that the Ternate had succeeded in anchoring in sight of the island; which she was only enabled to do by a fortuitous slant of wind for an hour or two. Had we been unfortunate in any one of these circumstances, few would have remained to tell our tale.

It is a tribute due to captain Maxwell to state (and it is a tribute which all most cheerfully pay), that, by his judicious arrangements, we were preserved from all the horrors of anarchy and confusion. His measures inspired confidence and hope; whilst his personal example, in the hour of danger, gave courage and animation to all around him.

We arrived at Batavia on the 9th, and, from the Ternate being so small, a number of our party crossed in the boats, which kept company with the ship. On the 10th we landed, and were most kindly received by lord Amherst, who converted his table into a general mess for the officers, as well as the embassy. Comfortable quarters were also provided for the men*, who, in a day or two, landed, and marched up there, with the flag which had been saved. They were met at Ryswick by his lordship, who accompanied them up. At Weltevreden, also, the officers met with a small, but choice band of their countrymen, whose society will not be easily forgotten, nor ever remembered without pleasure.

A short journal of lieutenant Cooke describes the passage of the embassy across the Javanese sea, in the boats.—" At seven in the evening of Wednesday, the 19th of February, all arrangements having been speedily made, the barge and cutter weighed, and pulled out to seaward, there being a heavy swell across the reef;—soon after made sail,

* The hospitable houses of Messrs. Milne and Terino afforded lodging to the officers during their stay; and much kind attention was experienced from captains Forbes, Dalgains, Hanson, and M'Mahon, of the staff of sir William Keir.

and sounded in nineteen fathoms;—kept more to the southward, having got into mid-channel;—at nine at night, entrance point, in the island of Banca, bore west three or four miles.

"Thursday, the 20th.—At day-light, the cutter in company; moderate breezes at W. N. W., and fair, with a smooth sea; high land of Banca bearing north;—having been much crowded in the night, some shifted into the other boat, in order to equalize the numbers. At seven, served out, for the first time, some provisions: a small portion of fresh meat and biscuit, with a gill of water and half a gill of rum, to each person. At ten a heavy squall occurred, attended by rain, which enabled us, by spreading cloths, and wringing them, to catch a bucket of rain-water, affording, to each person, about half a pint. Light airs, and calm: occasionally found it necessary to pull eight oars, and, by the assistance of the marines, we had two reliefs. Spelled the oars every two hours. Served out provisions and grog in the usual small proportions. Lowered the sails, the wind being adverse, afterwards becoming calm, and at other times light breezes from the south-west: each person had about half a pint of beer. Lightning from west to south-west,—water very smooth,—midnight, light airs.

"Friday, the 21st.—Moderate breezes from the westward, which soon became squally, and more to the southward, occasioning a swell of the sea. At seven o'clock served out the remains of the fresh meat, and the usual gill of water, and half a gill of rum. Examined stock after breakfast, and found remaining six gallons of water; spruce beer, eight gallons; rum, four gallons and a half; beer, four gallons; wine, nineteen bottles; five ditto of additional water, one ham, one tongue, and thirty pounds of bread. Served out, at twelve o'clock, some spruce to all hands. In the afternoon, served grog in the usual quantity. Continued rowing all night, and gave some spruce beer to the rowers, who began to be much fatigued. Wind variable from west to south-west.

"Saturday the 22d.—Continued pulling all this morning, the breeze being very light; mustered provisions, and found them much reduced. At seven o'clock issued grog and a little bread to each, reserving a ham, the only meat now remaining, until *dinner time*. All the gentlemen who could pull relieved the rowers. About one o'clock a favourable breeze sprung up at N. W. made all sail, and at half-past three o'clock saw Carawang Point, in Java, distant about nine or ten miles. At six o'clock the land-breeze coming off obliged the boats to anchor. Served out part of the ham, and a little biscuit and grog, as usual. At seven the wind moderated a little, and an attempt was made to row in; but, the people being nearly exhausted, anchored again at nine o'clock; the cutter having no grapnel, made fast to the barge. The night was fine, but a heavy swell occasioned the boat to roll extremely.

"Sunday morning the 23d, the people having had some repose, and a little refreshment served out to them, weighed the grapnel, and pulled towards Batavia. Between the two points of land here, we accidentally fell in, although at a considerable distance from the shore, with a stream of fresh water running into the sea, which put all in high spirits. To prevent any ill consequences, a little rum was put into a bucket, and every man drank about a pint. A favourable breeze also sprung up, and at half past ten o'clock we went along side the ship Princess Charlotte, in the roads, where we were very kindly received, our stock of provisions for forty-seven being at this time four or five pounds of bread, and (previous to falling in with the stream of fresh water in the sea), one gallon of water, one gallon of rum, and five bottles of wine, with some Madeira in a jar." During the whole of this little voyage the strictest equality was observed in the distribution of provisions; and if any distinction was made it was in favour of the rowers, those gentlemen who were unable to pull themselves taking a rather smaller proportion than those who did.

The circumstance of the stream of fresh water,

which seemed so providentially to extend into the sea, and afforded so much relief, is found to exist in many parts of the world, and has been lately turned to advantage by our Toulon fleet, which was enabled to water at the mouth of the Rhone, almost without losing sight of the port they were blockading.

Off the Mississippi, ships can water even out of sight of land; and the same is stated to be the case with the Oronoco, in South America. This will most probably be found in all narrow-mouthed rivers, which burst suddenly on the sea; and from the fresh being specifically lighter than the salt water, it naturally floats on the surface of the heavier body, and remains unmixed as long as the current retains its force.

The chief discomfort of this boat-voyage proceeded from being so crowded, and being obliged to sit so long in a particular posture, and the great distress arising from thirst. It was very difficult indeed to prevent the people from drinking salt water; one man became delirious, and it was attributed to this cause. It most probably, however, proceeded from the extreme irritation occasioned by thirst; for salt water, although an article of *materia medica* in very extensive use, has never been known to take the direction of the head.

About the 21st March the ship Charlotte returned to Batavia, which had sailed in company with the Ternate, having on board Messrs. Mayne, Blair, and Marrige. After beating against wind and current, from the 24th February to the 16th March, without being able to fetch farther than the south-east end of Banca, the current constantly sweeping them to leeward the moment they opened the Straits, Mr. Mayne, finding nothing was to be done in the ship, resolved to shove off in the barge, accompanied by the above gentlemen, and Mr. Thompson the supercargo, with two casks of water and one of beef for us, in the event of being still on the island. They tugged at the oars until the next day, when, arriving in sight of the place we had occupied, they found a large flotilla of the pirates at anchor there, three of whom immediately gave chase to our boat. There was no time to be lost; the barge made sail; but, in addition to their sails, the Malays pulled furiously, and were gaining fast. The beef and water were now thrown overboard, to lighten the barge; and, knowing whom they had to deal with, they prepared, being tolerably armed, to sell themselves as dear as possible. Fortunately at this moment a strong squall occurred, which compelled the Malays to lower their sails, whilst the barge, carrying through all, got a-head and escaped, the pirates hauling their wind again towards the island.

These proas were probably of the more distant islands, who, having only lately heard of the wreck, had arrived a day after the fair, and were hungry, and annoyed at finding no prey.

Nothing could exceed the deplorable state of Java at the period of its conquest by the British forces in 1811. The natives had at all times been enslaved and oppressed by the Dutch colonists; and, from the strict blockade of our cruizers, the produce of the soil which they were unable to export was rotting in the warehouses, and reducing the latter to a state of bankruptcy.

The system of government immediately introduced by lord Minto, under the able superintendence of Mr. Raffles, corresponding with that existing in British (and what is here termed western) India, very much altered the state of affairs; but it more especially ameliorated the condition of the native Javanese. It had been usual to compel the people to labour at the public works, whenever occasion required, without any, or at least for a very inadequate, remuneration. They were also obliged to deliver in a certain quantity of produce, often exceeding what they were able to afford; whilst they were tyrannically restricted to the cultivation of those articles only which best answered the purposes of the Dutch monopolists. By the new order of things these forced services were immediately abolished. The people were paid a reasonable price for their voluntary labour; and, instead of arbitrary and compulsory deliveries, encouragement was given to grow what were considered the most valuable productions of the island, and the Javanese were now stimulated to exertion by having an interest in the fruits of their industry. The revenue was now raised (except in one or two immaterial instances, which could not at once be conveniently altered) by a moderate land-tax on the whole. The rajahs or regents of the different districts were allowed (and indeed preferred) a fixed salary to abandon their claims, to the former harsh method of raising their incomes, whilst they were still intrusted under proper surveillance with the administration of the laws, which were also new-modelled and rendered more equitable, torture being abolished, and the instruments burnt in the public square. The Chinese farmers of revenue, employed under the Dutch, who possessed peculiar ingenuity in *squeezing* the natives, were either removed, or their conduct narrowly inspected by the British residents*.

* Sir T. Raffles, in his élaborate work on Java, states, "that whenever the Chinese formed extensive settlements in Java, the native inhabitants had no alternative but that of abandoning the district, or of becoming slaves of the soil. Their monopolizing spirit was often even pernicious to the produce, as may be seen even at this day in the immediate vicinity of Batavia, where all the public markets are farmed by them, and the degeneracy and poverty of the lower classes are proverbial."

In Java there is no interruption to the course of vegetation. The spring is eternal; and it is quite usual on the same day to see them sowing in one field, the second in half blossom, and reaping in the third. But with all these advantages of soil and climate the people had been driven to relinquish their native villages, and even to destroy the trees which the cruel impolicy of the whites compelled them to cultivate equally against their interest and their inclination.

In the first settlement of colonies, it is notorious that enormities were committed by *all* Europeans on the aborigines of the country; but without flattering our *amour propre national*, this unconciliatory and overbearing system seems to have been far less practised by us than by other nations, if we may judge from the comparative personal security with which a Briton roams every where at large. Previous to our possession of Java (when travelling became even more safe than in England), no Dutchman ever ventured to undertake a journey among the natives without a guard. The same is the case with the Portuguese and the original Brazilians, as well as the Spaniards at Manilla, and throughout the whole island of Luconia.

With the Javanese harsh and rigorous measures seem, and indeed have been clearly proved to be, as unnecessary as they are unjustifiable, for few people bear a more mild, docile, or inoffensive character. They are a distinct race from the Malays of the coasts, not only speaking a different language, but are anxious not to be confounded with them. Lord Minto, who was at Java at the period of its falling into our possession, made the following observations on the existing state of affairs, and the alterations he judged necessary :—

" Contingents of rice, and, indeed, of other productions, have been hitherto required of the cultivators, by government, at an arbitrary rate; this, also, is a vicious system, to be abandoned as soon as possible. The system of contingents did not arise from the mere solicitude for the people, but was a measure alone of finance and control, to enable government to derive a revenue from a high price imposed on the consumer, and to keep the whole body of the people dependent on its pleasure for subsistence. I recommend a radical reform in this branch to the serious and early attention of government. The principle of encouraging industry in the cultivation and improvement of lands, by creating an interest in the effort and fruits of that industry, can be expected in Java only by a fundamental change of the whole system of landed property and tenure. A wide field, but a somewhat distant one, is open to this great and interesting improvement; the discussion of the subject, however, must necessarily be delayed till the investigation it requires is more complete. I shall transmit

2 B

such thoughts as I have entertained, and such hopes as I have indulged, on this grand object of amelioration; but I am to request the aid of all the information, and all the lights, that this island can afford. On this branch, nothing must be done that is not mature, because the change is too extensive to be suddenly or ignorantly attempted. But fixed and immutable principles of the human character, and of human association, assure me of ultimate, and, I hope, not remote, success, in views that are consonant with every motive of action that operates on man, and are justified by the practice and experience of every flourishing country of the world!"

The wisdom and sound policy of these liberal and enlightened views have been fully proved by the increasing happiness and prosperity of the colony, from the day they were practically adopted, up to the period of the transfer of the island; and that the same system should be continued under the restored government appears to be the decided opinion of the wisest and most clear-sighted of the Dutch colonists; as well for its obvious justice and humanity, as from a conviction of its superior efficacy in every other respect.

At the same time measures were taken to abolish slavery, for the continuance of which, in Java, there appeared not even the plea of expediency. The farther importation of slaves was forbidden (for they were generally brought, for obvious reasons, from the neighbouring islands), and regulations were formed for the protection and better treatment of those actually existing. They were not allowed, for instance, to be sold or transferred from one master to another, but with their own approbation; they were permitted the right of acquiring property either by their own industry, or from the gifts of others, independent of the control of their masters, which they might appropriate, if they thought proper, after a certain term, to the purchase of their freedom, at a reasonable valuation, subject to the approval of a magistrate. An annual registry of each slave was also required, and a tax laid upon that registry, the proceeds of which were applied to charitable purposes; and, in any instance where this registry was omitted to be given in, the slave was declared free.

Although their present religion is that of Mahomet (with a mixture of Paganism), yet the numerous relics of Hinduism, in high preservation throughout the island, evidently shew that the latter was the original mode of worship. Indeed, Balli, one of the neighbouring islands, performs the Hindu rites at this day.

Batavia is considered, and with much reason, as one of the most unhealthy spots in the world. But this character is applicable only to the town itself; which, agreeably to Dutch usage, wherever they could find one, is built in a swamp. The effect of this, within seven degrees of the equator, is precisely what might be expected; but at Ryswick and Weltevreden, where the ground rises, certainly, not above a dozen or fifteen feet, and situated within three miles of the town, health is retained, at least, as perfectly as in any other part of India; and it has been even said that a battalion of a regiment quartered there has returned a smaller sick report than the other, stationed in some part of England. No European, who can possibly avoid it, ever sleeps in the city; but, after transacting his business, removes to the neighbourhood. Among seamen and soldiers, a night or two spent in Batavia is deemed mortal; but this increased fatality among them proceeds evidently from their never sleeping there but for the express purpose of getting drunk; and, when immersion in putrid and marsh effluvia, in so hot a climate, is applied to a body, rendered highly susceptible of their impression from previous ebriety, it is not to be wondered that a fever of the worst class should be the consequence. They are also not so likely, in these cases, to receive that prompt assistance which alone can save them; for, conscious of having been irregular in their conduct, they are ashamed and unwilling to make application until it is often too late; and the loss of a single day will, in severer cases, be attended, in all probability, with the most dangerous consequences*. The insalubrity of Batavia is attributed, but with little appearance of justice, to the numerous canals which intersect the town; for they rather seem to do good, by acting as drains, in a marshy soil; and, if they are the receptacles of filth and carcasses (which appeared not to be the case), it is the fault of the police, and not of the canals. Rice-fields, creating an artificial swamp, in addition to the natural moisture of the ground, certainly ought not to be permitted to exist in the immediate vicinity of a populous city; and cannot be at all necessary in a country, two-thirds of which is uncultivated.

The climate of Java may be varied at pleasure, from the suffocating heat of Bantam, or Batavia, to the cool, and even keen, air of the mountains, where fires and blankets are necessary; which, to invalids requiring an immediate change of temperature, is an advantage of the highest importance.

It is extraordinary how defective all colonies are in seminaries of education;—a defect, more espe-

* Captain Charles Ross, of the Pique, in the West Indies, among other judicious regulations of that excellent officer (whose orders were neither multiplied nor confused, and, for that reason, more likely to be rational), always considered a man found drunk to be an object for the surgeon's immediate care, in the first instance; and it is astonishing the good effect this had, not only in preventing drunkenness, but in obviating its effects.

cially in those that are extensive and populous, for which there can be no good excuse, and is attended with much inconvenience; for either the youth of both sexes receive no education at all, or must be sent home, at a great expense, for that purpose. This would appear to be much the case at Batavia, for the young men required to fill situations of responsibility must be supplied by fresh importations; and the ladies, surrounded by a crowd of flattering slave-girls, generally *creolize** the whole day in a delectable state of apathy, without any sort of occupation; at sun-set, perhaps, taking a short airing in the environs. The elder dames inveterately adhere to the *kubaya* (a loose sort of gown, or wrapper, sometimes richly embroidered), but the English and French modes are universal among the rising generation. They form a curious contrast on public occasions, for, although sumptuary laws exist, which prevent, more especially ladies, from wearing jewels beyond a certain amount, and appearing abroad attended by servants exceeding the number allowed for the particular rank of their husbands or fathers; yet all classes, male and female,

* Creolizing is an easy and elegant mode of lounging in a warm climate; so called, because much in fashion among the ladies of the West Indies: that is, reclining back in one arm-chair, with their feet upon another, and sometimes upon the table.

seem privileged to *undress* themselves as they please.

One evening, on our passage outwards, at a grand ball given by the British army officers, on the anniversary of the battle of Waterloo, at the Harmonie, an elderly gentleman, in a full suit of black, highly trimmed, and in the cut of the last century, was seen strutting about the room with a white night-cap on his head. Indeed, at dinner, in the best companies, they do not hesitate to wear their hats, if there is the least motion in the air; for they dread nothing so much as sitting in a current.

The villas of the counsellors of the Indies are distinguished by having black instead of white statues in their fronts, and about their gardens. They are, generally, heavy-looking houses, situated on the Jacatra and Ryswick roads, but have an air of stateliness.

The restored Dutch government professes to act upon the principles which have been found successful during our possession; but a circumstance which occurred a short time before our arrival here evinced strong symptoms of a recurrence to the system of terror. A body of the natives, about five hundred in number, having had some dispute with the local authorities near Indra Mayo, whilst making representation about some hardship (which they had been lately freely in the habit of doing, whenever they considered themselves in any way aggrieved), were seized, and confined in a house, which, like the black hole of Calcutta, being too small for the prisoners, they, in desperation, attempted to break through the roof; when a body of military having by this time been collected, they were fired upon, the greater part killed, and the remainder, in some way or other, destroyed. It is somewhat extraordinary that the Dutch, who are, at home, a very unassuming, plain, and moral sort of people, should have displayed, on so many occasions, a ferocious and blood-thirsty disposition in their colonies. Marshal Daendels, it is confessed, made many judicious arrangements by the vigour of his measures, had he only been a little more scrupulous as to the mode of obtaining his purposes; but, to use his own expression, he "found it necessary to put himself above the usual formalities, and to disregard every law but that which enjoined the preservation of the colony intrusted to his management."

On one occasion he is said to have requested the magistrates to demolish their grand church in Batavia, which was not only in the way of some favourite scheme he had in view, but its cupola was the only land-mark for entering the bay, and, as such, greatly assisted the enemy's cruizers. The burgomasters ventured to oppose this project. In a very short time the church was found to be on fire; and the building being thereby in a great degree consumed and damaged, the remainder was soon razed to the ground*. His great military road, carried some hundred miles across the island, cost the lives of thousands of the Javanese, who were sacrificed to the system of forced services. He appears to have been little less despotic with the whites ; and many stories are told about him, " that he could even make hens lay eggs when he thought proper ;" but, although all seem to agree that he carried a high and imperious hand, yet none dare, even now, speak ill of him, for fear he may return.

In equipping a considerable army, merely from the resources of the country, when entirely cut off from any communication with Europe, supplying them with a cloth adapted to the climate, and furnishing them with most of the other accoutrements, he put the manufacturing talents of the natives to the test, and he succeeded.

Sir William Keir, Mr. Fendal, and Mr. Cranssen, were still at Batavia, for the purpose of finally adjusting the transfer of the colonies, with the commissioners of his majesty, the king of the Netherlands. The Dutch squadron was absent at the different islands, resuming possession of them. They had, as well as the land-forces, suffered a very heavy loss from deaths ; and the baron de Capellan, who is individually a man of humanity, and was

* The incendiaries were never found out.

extremely solicitous about their preservation, was stated to have personally interfered with the medical staff, who appear to have been much wedded to the old-fashioned practice, and to have given positive orders that the mode of managing the sick, which had proved successful with our troops on the very same ground, should be adhered to.

The ship Cæsar, captain Taylor, having been engaged to carry to England the embassy, with the officers and crew of the Alceste, being now ready for sea, her equipment having been expedited by the assistance of our artificers, his lordship embarked on the 12th of April, attended by sir William Keir, and all his staff, and receiving, from the Dutch authorities, every mark of respect due to his rank. We sailed on the same morning, and soon cleared the Straits of Sunda, and proceeded with a fair wind across the Indian Ocean.

The gay scenes we had experienced for the last few weeks among our friends at Weltevreden and Batavia, and which we had enjoyed with the greater spirit from our previous adventures, made us more susceptible of the dull sameness attending our present *sky-and-water* view. But a circumstance occurred, of all others producing the most instantaneous and effectual relief from this feeling of *tedium vitæ* or *ennui*. The ship, one morning, was declared to be on fire in the after store-room, and (to render the intelligence still more agreeable and interésting) close to the magazine, whilst the flames seen in that direction, and volumes of smoke now bursting forth, left no doubt of the fact. In a moment the liveliest bustle took place of listless yawning, and every mind was roused into a state of the highest activity. To be in a ship on fire in the middle of the ocean is supposed to be the most awkward and unenviable situation in which a man of weak nerves can be placed. Some again assert that it affords, more than any other occasion, an opportunity for the display of coolness, presence of mind, and decision. Happily, there were not wanting many possessing the latter qualities, who, by pushing through the smoke to the point of danger, and scuttling the decks immediately above the place, succeeded in extinguishing the flames in about three quarters of an hour, but not without considerable difficulty and damage. Very fortunately it was washing morning, and, of course, buckets, and other water utensils, were at hand. Had the accident taken place during the night, or had it been unobserved for a few minutes longer, and the fire had communicated to some oil and other combustibles near it, no human power could have saved us. This alarming occurrence, so nearly proving fatal, was occasioned by an idle looby, belonging to the Cæsar, carelessly pumping off spirits with a naked light, in order to preserve the body of *a parrot*, which had died the night before. It had the effect, however, of occasioning the most rigorous precautions in future.

Notwithstanding the crowded state of the Cæsar, two passengers, of rather a singular nature, were put on board at Batavia, for a passage to England: the one, a snake of that species called Boa Constrictor: the other, an Ourang Outang.—The former was somewhat small of his kind, being only about sixteen feet long, and of about eighteen inches in circumference; but his stomach was rather disproportionate to his size, as will presently appear.—He was a native of Borneo, and was the property of a gentleman (now in England), who had two of the same sort; but, in their passage up to Batavia, one of them broke loose from his confinement, and very soon cleared the decks, as every body very civilly made way for him. Not being used to a ship, however, or taking, perhaps, the sea for a green field, he sprawled overboard, and was drowned. He is said not to have sunk immediately, but to have reared his head several times, and with it a considerable portion of his body, out of the sea. His companion, lately our shipmate, was brought safely on shore, and lodged in the court-yard of Mr. Davidson's house at Ryswick, where he remained for some months, waiting for an opportunity of being conveyed home in some commodious ship sailing directly for England, and where he was likely to be carefully attended to.

This opportunity offered in the Cæsar, and he was accordingly embarked on board of that ship with the rest of her numerous passengers.

During his stay at Ryswick he is said to have been usually entertained with a goat for dinner once in every three or four weeks, with occasionally a duck or a fowl, by way of a desert.—He was brought on board shut up in a wooden crib or cage, the bars of which were sufficiently close to prevent his escape; and it had a sliding door, for the purpose of admitting the articles on which he was to subsist; the dimensions of the crib were about four feet high, and about five feet square; a space sufficiently large to allow him to coil himself round with ease. The live stock for his use during the passage, consisting of six goats of the ordinary size, were sent with him on board, five being considered as a fair allowance for as many months. At an early period of the voyage we had an exhibition of his talent in the way of eating, which was publicly performed on the quarter-deck, upon which he was was brought. The sliding door being opened, one of the goats was thrust in, and the door of the cage shut. The poor goat, as if instantly aware of all the horrors of its perilous situation, immediately began to utter the most piercing and distressing cries, butting instinctively, at the same time, with its head towards the serpent, in self-defence.

The snake, which at first appeared scarcely to notice the poor animal, soon began to stir a little, and, turning his head in the direction of the goat, it at length fixed a deadly and malignant eye on the trembling victim, whose agony and terror seemed to increase; for, previous to the snake seizing its prey, it shook in every limb, but still continuing its unavailing show of attack, by butting at the serpent, who now became sufficiently animated to prepare for the banquet. The first operation was that of darting out his forked tongue, and at the same time rearing a little his head; then suddenly seizing the goat by the fore leg with his mouth, and throwing him down, he was encircled in an instant in his horrid folds. So quick, indeed, and so instantaneous was the act, that it was impossible for the eye to follow the rapid convolution of his elongated body. It was not a regular *screw-like* turn that was formed, but resembling rather a knot, one part of the body overlaying the other, as if to add weight to the muscular pressure, the more effectually to crush his object. During this time he continued to grasp with his mouth, though it appeared an unnecessary precaution, that part of the animal which he had first seized. The poor goat, in the mean time, continued its feeble and *half-stifled* cries for some minutes, but they soon became more and more faint, and at last it expired. The snake, however, retained it for a considerable time in its grasp, after it was apparently motionless. He then began slowly and cautiously to unfold himself, till the goat fell dead from his monstrous embrace, when he began to prepare himself for the feast. Placing his mouth in front of the head of the dead animal, he commenced by lubricating with his saliva that part of the goat; and then taking its muzzle into his mouth, which had, and indeed always has, the appearance of a raw lacerated wound, he *sucked it in*, as far as the horns would allow. These protuberances opposed some little difficulty, not so much from their extent as from their points; however, they also, in a very short time, disappeared; that is to say, externally; but their progress was still to be traced very distinctly on the outside, threatening every moment to protrude through the skin. The victim had now descended as far as the shoulders; and it was an astonishing sight to observe the extraordinary action of the snake's muscles when stretched to such an unnatural extent—an extent which must have utterly destroyed all muscular power in any animal that was not, like itself, endowed with very peculiar faculties of expansion and action at the same time. When his head and neck had no other appearance than that of a serpent's skin stuffed almost to bursting, still the workings of the muscles were evident; and his power of suction, as it is erroneously called, unabated; it was, in fact, the effect of a contractile muscular power, assisted by two rows of strong hooked teeth. With all this he must be so formed as to be able to suspend, for a time, his respiration, for it is impossible to conceive that the process of breathing could be carried on while the mouth and throat were so completely stuffed and expanded by the body of the goat, and the lungs themselves (admitting the trachea to be ever so hard) compressed, as they must have been, by its passage downwards.

The whole operation of completely gorging the goat occupied about two hours and twenty minutes: at the end of which time, the tumefaction was confined to the middle part of the body, or stomach, the superior parts, which had been so much distended, having resumed their natural dimensions. He now coiled himself up again, and lay quietly in his usual torpid state for about three weeks or a month, when his last meal appearing to be completely digested and dissolved, he was presented with another goat, which he devoured with equal facility. It would appear that almost all he swallows is converted into nutrition, for a small quantity of calcareous matter (and that, perhaps, not a tenth part of the bones of the animal) with occasionally some of the hairs, seemed to compose his *general* fæces;—and this may account for these animals being able to remain so long without a supply of food. He had more difficulty in killing a fowl than a larger animal, the former being too small for his grasp.

Few of those who had witnessed his first exhibition were desirous of being present at the second. A man may be impelled by curiosity, and a wish to ascertain the truth of a fact frequently stated, but which seems almost incredible, to satisfy his own mind by ocular proof; but he will leave the scene with those feelings of horror and disgust, which such a sight is well calculated to create. It is difficult to behold, without the most painful sensation, the anxiety and trepidation of the harmless victim, or to observe the hideous writhing of the serpent around his prey, and not to imagine what our own case would be in the same helpless and dreadful situation.

A lion, a tiger, and other beasts of prey, are sufficiently terrible; but they seldom, unless strongly urged by hunger, attack human beings, and generally give some sort of warning; but, against the silent, sly, and insiduous approach of a snake, there is no guarding, nor any escape when once entwined within his folds.

As we approached the Cape of Good Hope, this animal began to droop, as was then supposed, from the increasing coldness of the weather (which may probably have had its influence), and he refused to kill some fowls which were offered to him. Be-

2 D

tween the Cape and St. Helena he was found dead in his cage; and, on dissection, the coats of his stomach were discovered to be excoriated and perforated by worms. Nothing remained of the goat except one of the horns, every *other part* being dissolved.

It may here be mentioned, that, during a captivity of some months at Whidah, in the kingdom of Dahomey, on the coast of Africa, the author of this narrative had opportunities of observing snakes more than double the size of this one just described; but he cannot venture to say whether or not they were of the same species, though he has no doubt of their being of the genus Boa. They killed their prey, however, precisely in a similar manner; and, from their superior bulk, were capable of swallowing animals much larger than goats or sheep. Governor Abson, who had for thirty-seven years resided at Fort William (one of the African company's settlements here), described some desperate struggles which he had either seen, or came to his knowledge, between the snakes and wild beasts, as well as the smaller cattle, in which the former were always victorious. A negro herdsman belonging to Mr. Abson (who afterwards limped for many years about the fort) had been seized by one of these monsters by the thigh; but, from his situation in a wood, the serpent, in attempting to throw itself around him, got entangled with a tree; and the man, being thus preserved from a state of compression which would have instantly rendered him quite powerless, had presence of mind enough to cut with a large knife, which he carried about with him, deep gashes in the neck and throat of his antagonist, thereby killing it, and disengaging himself from his alarming situation. He never afterwards, however, recovered the use of that limb, which had sustained considerable injury from his fangs, and the mere force of his jaws.

These larger reptiles are seldom observed to be venomous, the smaller tribe being, in this respect, much more dangerous.

In this country they had a smaller species of snake, called *Daboa*, which is the object of their worship and adoration. It is perfectly harmless (to larger creatures), and is tameable. Great attention is paid to any that are found, being lodged in their temples, and fed by the priestesses with rats, mice, and smaller animals. People who are sick apply to it for relief; and, should one of them happen to entwine itself around a pregnant woman, it is considered the happiest possible omen for herself and child. In this state she proudly marches through the town, sanctified, as it were, by the attachment of the snake, which encircles her naked frame; and followed by crowds, those who meet her falling on their knees, and snapping their fingers (the usual salutation) as she passes.

The Ourang Outang, also a native of Borneo, is an animal remarkable not only from being extremely rare, but as possessing, in many respects, a strong resemblance to man. What is technically denominated the cranium is perfectly human in its appearance; the shape of the upper part of the head, the forehead, the eyes (which are dark and full), the eye-lashes, and, indeed, every thing relating to the eyes and ears, differing in no respect from man. The hair of his head, however, is merely the same which covers his body generally. The nose is very flat,—the distance between it and the mouth considerable; the chin, and, in fact, the whole of the lower jaw, is very large, and his teeth, twenty-six in number, are strong. The lower part of his face is what may be termed an ugly, or caricature, likeness of the human countenance. The position of the scapulæ, or shoulder blades, the general form of the shoulders and breasts, as well as the figure of the arms, the elbow-joint especially, and the hands, strongly continue the resemblance. The metacarpal, or that part of the hand immediately above the fingers, is somewhat elongated; and, by the thumb being thrown a little higher up, nature seems to have adapted the hand to his mode of life, and given him the power of grasping more effectually the branches of trees.

He is corpulent about the abdomen, or, in common phrase, rather *pot-bellied*, looking like one of those figures of Bacchus often seen riding on casks; but whether this is his natural appearance when wild, or acquired since his introduction into new society, and by indulging in a high style of living, it is difficult to determine.

His thighs and legs are short and bandy, the ankle and heel like the human; but the fore part of the foot is composed of toes, as long and as pliable as his fingers, with a thumb a little situated before the inner ankle; this conformation enabling him to hold equally fast with his feet as with his hands. When he stands erect he is about three feet high, and he can walk, when led, like a child; but his natural locomotion, when on a plane surface, is supporting himself along, at every step, by placing the knuckles of his hands upon the ground. All the fingers, both of the hands and feet, have nails exactly like the human race, except the thumb of the foot, which is without any.

His natural food would appear to be all kinds of fruit and nuts; but he eats biscuit, or any other sort of bread, and sometimes animal food. He will drink grog, or even spirits, if given to him; and has been known repeatedly to help himself in this way: he was also taught to sip his tea or coffee, and since his arrival in England, has discovered a taste for a pot of porter. His usual conduct is not mischievous, and chattering like that of monkeys in general; but he has rather a grave and sedate character, and is much inclined to be social, and on good terms, with every body. He made no difficulty, however, when cold, or inclined to sleep, in supplying himself with any jacket he found hanging about, or in stealing a pillow from a hammock, in order to lie more soft and comfortably.

Sometimes, when teased by shewing him something to eat, he would display in a very strong manner the human passions, following the person whining and crying, throwing himself off on his back, and rolling about apparently in a great rage, attempting to bite those near him, and frequently lowering himself by a rope over the ship's side, as if pretending to drown himself; but, when he came near the water's edge, he always reconsidered the matter, and came on board again. He would often rifle and examine the pockets of his friends in quest of nuts and biscuits, which they sometimes carried for him. He had a great antipathy to the smaller tribe of monkeys, and would throw them overboard if he could; but in his general habits and disposition there is much docility and good nature, and, when not annoyed, he is extremely inoffensive. He approaches, upon the whole, nearer to the human kind than any other animal.

On the 27th May we anchored in Simon's Bay, at the Cape of Good Hope, from which we sailed again on the 11th of June, steering for St. Helena, where we arrived on the 27th. The exterior of this island has much of that appearance which induced madame Bertrand to term it the birth-place of the demon of Ennui; but the interior is not destitute of beauties, for there are many very pleasing spots situated in its different valleys.

One cannot help, in contemplating the calm tranquillity which reigns about Longwood (now the peaceful habitation of the greatest agitator of the world), being forcibly struck by the great mutability of human affairs.

Bonaparte had for a considerable time past been very retired and difficult of access, but he was perfectly disposed to see lord Amherst; and on the day previous to our departure his lordship rode out there, accompanied by the gentlemen of his suite. He was introduced by Bertrand with not a little form, and had, as well as Mr. Ellis, a very long private conversation previous to the introduction of the other gentlemen, who in the mean time were attended by generals Bertrand, Montholon, and Gourgaud, in the next room. At last they also were ushered in; and a ring having been formed by the marshal round the principal personage of the group, Lord Amherst presented to him first captain Maxwell, to whom he bowed very civilly, and said his name was not unknown to him; observing, he had commanded on an occasion where one of his frigates, La Pomone, was taken in the Mediterranean. "*Vous étiez très mechant—Eh bien!* your government must not blame you for the loss of the Alceste, for you have taken one of my frigates." He said he was very happy to see young Jeffery Amherst, and good-humouredly asked him what presents he had brought with him from China, and so forth.

The author of this narrative he interrogated about the length of time he had served, and whether he had been wounded; repeating the last question in English.

Proceeding next to Mr. Abel (who was introduced as naturalist), he inquired if he belonged to the royal society, or any of the public institutions, or was a candidate for that honour; asking if he had been happy, in this voyage, in making any discoveries in natural history, which could add to our stock of knowledge on that subject. Whether he knew Sir Joseph Banks, whose name, he said, was a passport in France; and his wishes always attended to, even during war.

Mr. Cooke's name induced him to ask if he was a descendant of the celebrated navigator; observing, "You had a Cooke, who was, indeed, a great man." He requested to know, on Dr. Lynn being presented, at what university he had studied.—"At Edinburgh" was the reply.—"Edinboorg!" he repeated; and went on to interrogate him whether he was a Brunonian in practice; or if he bled and gave as much mercury as *our* St. Helena doctors.

Mr. Griffith, the chaplain, was next introduced, whom Buonaparte termed *l'aumonier*, and pronouncing, also, in English, *clair-gee-man.* "Well, sir," he continued, "have you found out what religion the Chinese profess?" Mr. G. replied it was somewhat difficult to say; but it seemed a sort of polytheism. Not appearing to understand the meaning of this word, spoken in English, Bertrand remarked "*Pluralité de Dieux.*"—"Ah! *pluralité de Dieux*," said he; "do they believe in the immortality of the soul?" "I think they have some idea of a future state," was the reply. "Well," said Buonaparte, "when you go home you must get a good living; I wish you may be made a prebendary, sir." Proceeding to Mr. Hayne, he also questioned him in some general way; and having now completed the circle, and said something to every body, he very courteously bowed to each of the party as they retired, who all felt much gratified at the opportunity of the interview. Although there was nothing *descending* in his manner, yet it was affable and polite; and, whatever may be his general habit, he can behave himself *very prettily* if he pleases. He is by no means so corpulent as is usually represented, and his health appears to be excellent. Longwood, from its situation, ought certainly to be highly salubrious. On the 2d of July we sailed from St. Helena, touched at the island of Ascension on the 7th, and, on

2 E

the 12th, crossed the line, and got into our own hemisphere. Our passage homewards was extremely favourable, on the 16th of August making the land, and the next morning brought us to Spithead, from whence we landed once more in our native isle; not merely with the common feeling of happiness which all mankind naturally enjoy on revisiting the land of their birth, but with those sensations of pride and satisfaction with which every Briton may look round him, in his own country, after having seen all others.

END OF THE NARRATIVE.

APPENDIX.

NO. I.

ON our arrival at Portsmouth, a court martial (as is usual in the navy) was held on board the Queen Charlotte, to inquire into all the circumstances attending the loss of the ship, and into the conduct of the officers and men on that occasion; composed of captain sir Archibald Dickson, bart. president; captains Alexander, Dacres, Meynell, and Hickey; Moses Greatham, judge advocate; when, after Captain Maxwell's interesting narrative, detailing the facts relative thereto, having been read, and a number of witnesses examined on the various statements contained in it, the court pronounced the following sentence, after the usual preamble :—

" Having maturely and deliberately weighed and considered the whole, the court is of opinion, that the loss of his majesty's late ship Alceste was caused by her striking on a sunken rock, until then unknown in the straits of Gaspar. That captain Murray Maxwell, previous to the circumstance, appeared to have conducted himself in the most zealous and officer-like manner; and, after the ship struck, his coolness, self-collection, and exertions, were highly conspicuous; and that every thing was done by him and his officers, within the power of man to execute, previous to the loss of the ship, and afterwards to preserve the lives of the right honourable lord Amherst, his majesty's embassador, and his suite, as well as those of the ship's company, and to save her stores on that occasion; and therefore adjudge the said captain Murray Maxwell, his officers and men, to be *most fully acquitted.*"

The court was very crowded, and there were present lords Amherst and Colchester. The former, being examined by the court, stated, "that he had selected captain Maxwell, on the occasion of the embassy, from motives of personal friendship, as well as from the high opinion he entertained of his professional character, which opinion had been much increased by the events of this voyage."

NO. II.

CHRONOLOGICAL LIST of the Kings of Lewchew, from the End of the Twelfth Century, to the Beginning of last.

NAMES OF KINGS.	First Year of their Reign.	Lived.	Duration of Reign.
	A. D.	Years.	Years.
Chun-tien	1187	72	51
Chun-Machuny, son of Chun-tien	1238	64	11
Ypen, son of Chun-Machuny	1249	—	—
Yn-tsou	1260	71	40
Ta-tching, son of Yn-tsou	1301	—	9
Yn-tse, second son of Ta-tching	1309	—	5
Yu-tching, fourth son of Yn-tse	1314	—	23
Ly-Oucy, son of Yu-tching	1337	23	14
Tsay-tou	1350	—	46
Ou-ning, son of Tsay-tou	1396	—	—
Tse-chaó, son of Ou-ning	1406	—	16
Chang-pa-tchi, son of Tse-chao	1424	68	18
Chang-tchong, second son of Chang-pa-tchi	1440	54	—
Chang-tse-ta, son of Chang-tchong	1445	42	5
Chang-kin-foo, paternal uncle of Chang-tse-ta	1450	52	4
Chang-tai-kieou, brother of Chang-kin-foo	1454	46	7

NAMES OF KINGS.	First Year of their Reign. A. D.	Lived. Years.	Duration of Reign. Years.
Chang-te, third son of Chang-ta-kieou	1461	29	9
Chang-y-ven	1470	62	7
Chang-tching, son of Chang-y-ven	1477	62	50
Chang-tsing, third son of Chang-tching	1527	59	29
Chang-y-ven, second son of Chang-tsing	1556	45	17
Chang-yong, second son of Chang-y-ven	1573	35	16
Chang-ning, grandson of Chang-tsing	1588	57	32
Chang-fong, descendant of a brother of Chang-yong	1621	51	20
Chang-hien, third son of Chang-fong	1641	23	7
Chang-tche, brother of Chang-hien	1648	40	21
Chang-tching, son of Chang-hien	1669	65	41
Chang-pen, grandson of Chang-tching	1710	34	3
Chang-king, son of Chang-pen	1713	—	—

The above list being copied, by père Gaubil, from the Chinese Report of Supoa-Koang, they have, in that translation from the original language, no doubt, acquired their present Chinese character of expression.

NO. III.

NAMES and SITUATION of the Lewchew Islands, according to the same authority.

To the North-eastward.

Yon-chang-pou
Fokou
Yeoula
Oa-kinou
Kia-ki-luma
Tatao (of considerable size)
Ki-ki-ai

To the South and Westward.

Typin-chan, or Ma-kou-chan
Ykima
Yleang-pa
Koulima
Talama
Mienna
Oukomi
Pat-chong-chan
Palouma
Yeouni Koumi
Kaumi
Te-ke-tou-non
Kauli-che-ma
Ola-ke-se-kou
Pa-tou-li-ma

To the North and Westward.

Gan-kini-chan
Kichan
Ye-Kichan
Lun-koan-chan (or Sulphur Island)
Mat-che-chan, surrounded by five islets
Another Mat-che-chan
Koumi-chan

To the Eastward.

Kon-ta-tia
Tsin-kinou
Ysi
Pama

The whole situate at various distances, extending from the main island towards Japan, Corea, and the island of Formosa, four only lying to the eastward.

NO. IV.

MR. FISHER collected a few of the Lewchewan words, which may tend to give some idea of the sound of their language.

Beard.	Figoo.
Button.	Tama.
Book.	Shumutsee.
Bite.	Quayon.
Boat with sails.	Tima.
Boat rowed with oars.	Chunee.
Branches of trees.	Tanun.
Comb.	Sabachee.
Chair.	Ee.
Cows.	Ooshu.
Cold.	Fuisa.
Cut.	Chichau.
Candle.	Doe.
Coffin.	Quan.
Come ashore.	Chung.
Cloth.	Dasha.
Colours (ensign).	Chuata.
Coral.	Ooru.
Come here.	Cuma cay-chung.
Day.	Okiou.
Drink.	Nummee.
Dead.	Sijoug.

Eye.	Me.
Egg.	Cooga.
Earth.	Sinna.
Eat.	Conun.
Fingers.	Ibec.
Feet.	Fisha.
Fowls.	Fuee.
Fan.	Ogee.
Fan-ning.	Ogee-shun.
Fish-ing.	Juh-shun.
Goat.	Figa.
Good.	Yutissa.
Grave (for dead).	Hacka.
Good bye, or adieu.	Wa-coutee.
God.	Joh.
Gong.	Caniutchung.
Hair.	Carasee.
Hat.	Camuree.
He.	Adee.
Handkerchief.	Sagee.
Horse.	Mah.
Head-pin with a star-head.	Camesashee.
Head-pin with a scoop-head.	Uaisashee.
How do you do?	Uga-ma-bidda?
Ink.	Tamagufing.
Jar.	Tusaadzee.
I or me.	Oau
I will come again.	Atucara.
I do not understand.	Chi-carang.
I thank you.	Ca-fush.
I will go.	Oa Atchung.
I will sing.	Oa Utahang.
Knife.	Sigu.

2 F

Large.	Ufishta.
Moon.	Stee.
Musquito.	Gadjang.
Milk.	Chee.
Man.	Ekegah.
Nose.	Hana.
Nails.	Cimee.
Night.	Masta.
Not good.	Wassa.
No.	Arang.
Oil.	Unda.
Paper.	Cabee.
Potatoes (sweet).	Moo.
Physician or Surgeon.	Isha.
Priest.	Bozy.
Pig.	Oa.
Rain.	Amuie.
Riding.	Ditaugin.
Sun.	Tida.
Stars.	Hushee.
Shoes.	Saba.
Stones.	Ishee.
Sit down.	Iree.
Ship (large).	Ufubuny.
Ship (small).	Cubunee.
Sleep.	Ninjun.
Sick.	Yadon.
Sailor.	Biotee.
Shell.	Keh.
Silk.	Dunsy.
Stone-mason.	Ichi-secu.
Square used by ditto.	Banjoganee.
Serpent.	Onegha.

Sea.	Ooshu.
Sand.	Sinna.
Sash or Girdle, worn by the Lewchewans.	Ubu.
Stop.	Ichuna.
Small.	Coosa.
Teeth.	Ha.
Trowsers.	Jacama.
Trees.	Ifcoojee.
Tobacco-pipe.	Tsidee.
To bring.	Toute-coo.
Tea.	Cha (Chinese.)
Temple, or house of worship in the garden, where the sick were.	Jah Joh.
Umbrella.	Cassa.
Very good.	Churissa.
Water.	Midzee.
Wind.	Casechute.
Wood.	Kee.
Woman.	Inago.
You.	Ya.
You give me.	Yare Curran.
Yes.	Simung.
You are a good fellow.	Churamung.

NUMERALS.

1 Titsee.
1 Tatsee.
3 Metsee.
4 Yutsee.
5 Ititsee.
6 Mutsee.
7 Nanatsee.
8 Jatsee.
9 Cucunutsee.
10 Too.
11 Too-Titsee.
12 Too-Tatsee, and so on to nineteen.
20 Nijoo.
21 Nijoo-Titsee, &c.
30 Sanjoo.
31 Sanjoo-Titsee, &c.
40 Sinjoo.
41 Sinjoo-Titsee, &c.
50 Gunjoo.
51 Gunjoo-Titsee, &c.
60 Docodoo.
61 Ducodoo-Titsee, &c.
70 Stigoo.
71 Stigoo-Titsee, &c.
80 Hacheegoo.
81 Hachegoo-Titsee, &c.
90 Cunjoo.
91 Cunjoo-Titsee, &c.
100 Hiacoo.

The numbers after each ten were always repeated in a manner similar to our own arithmetic.

No. V.

THE FAREWELL.

[*The insertion of the following verses, by Mr. Gillard, clerk of the Lyra, may not, perhaps, be deemed irrelevant to the subject, as they express not only his own, but the general sentiments, on leaving the worthy Islanders at Grand Lewchew.*]

THE sails are set,—the anchor weigh'd;
  Their course, south-west, the ships pursue;
And, friendly signs at parting made,
  We bid the land a last adieu!

From crowded boats, that grace our wake,
  In cap and vest but seldom wore,
Their last "FAREWELL" the natives take,
  And, half-reluctant, seek the shore.

Each cliff's rude height and sea-worn base
  Presents a silent gazing throng;
Where e'en regret may find a place,
  As swift the vessels pass along.

And now the harbour's far astern;
The dang'rous reefs in distance fade;—
No object can the eye discern
Without the glass's friendly aid.

Yet, while the anxious straining sight
Can still behold the fleeting shore,
The telescope shall yield delight,
And all its pleasing scenes restore.

Again the rocks and tombs appear,
The trees and straw-built huts arise,
Where constant guards were plac'd, by fear,
To screen each beauty from our eyes.

The path beside the wat'ring-place,
Where branching pines adorn the hill,
Th' assisted eye can faintly trace,
And mark its num'rous windings still.

There, too, the stone enclosure stands,
Within whose high extensive walls
The pagan native lifts his hands,
And on his wooden idol calls.

Yet ye, who boast the Christian name,
Blush at a deed which truth must tell:—
Hither they brought the sick and lame,
And bade them in their temples dwell.

From noise and crowded decks remov'd,
Th' infirm inhal'd a purer air;
And native kindness daily prov'd
They bless the hand that led them there.

In yonder grove's encircling shade,
Where time will long the truth attest,
The last sad rites by strangers paid,
A youthful seaman's ashes rest.

What tho' oblivion o'er his name
May spread her veil of deepest gloom,
Full many a fav'rite child of fame
Would not disdain an equal tomb.

Yet not the sick their thoughts confin'd,
Nor yet th' interment of the dead;
The living still they bore in mind,
And gave the ships their daily bread.

While friendship thus was shewn to all,
Congenial minds attach'd a few;
And mem'ry oft will, pleas'd, recall
The names of "Mad'ra," and "Geroo."

Farewell, dear isle!—on you may breath
Of civil discord never blow!
Far from your shores be plague and death,
And far—oh! far—the hostile foe!

To distant climes our course we steer,
Where fashion boasts her splendid reign;
Where science, fame, and wealth, appear,
While lux'ry revels in their train.

Meanwhile, ne'er 'mid your smiling scenes
May pride and fierce ambition spring!
Ne'er may they know what mis'ry means,
Which vice and dissipation bring!

Still on your sons may plenty shine,
  Still may their happiness increase;
And friendship long their hearts entwine
  With love, with innocence, and peace.

No more;—for now the fresh'ning breeze
  Impels us swiftly o'er the deep;
Your verdant shores no longer please,
  And faint appear your mountains steep.

Their summits now are cloth'd in gray,
  And scarce the eye their place can tell;
And now they're melted quite away,—
  Once more, DEAR ISLAND, FARE THEE WELL!

THE END.

(3)

Oct. 1817.

MODERN PUBLICATIONS,

AND

NEW EDITIONS

OF

VALUABLE STANDARD WORKS,

PRINTED FOR

M. CAREY & SON, No. 126, CHESNUT STREET, PHILADELPHIA.

VOYAGES, TRAVELS, GEOGRAPHY, AND TOPOGRAPHY.

TRAVELS IN BRAZIL. By HENRY KOSTER.
In 2 vols. 8vo. Price 4 dollars, boards.

Of this work the Quarterly Review for January 1817, says:

"The general spirit of the book, indeed, is excellent; the manner more resembling the good, old, plain, straight forward style of our best travellers, than the modern fashion of fine periods; and the matter for the most part equally curious and amusing, presenting a faithful picture of a very interesting stage, in the progress of society."

A JOURNEY THROUGH ALBANIA, and other Provinces of Turkey in Europe and Asia, to Constantinople; in the years 1809 and 1810. By J. C. HOBHOUSE.
In 2 vols. 8vo. with a 4to. vol. of plates. Price 8 dolls. in boards.

"These volumes are the work of a person very active and observant, very intelligent, and largely furnished with the pre-requisites for travelling in the classical regions." *Eclectic Review.*

"The work will fully merit a stand and place in all collections of voyages and travels, by the industry and order of research conspicuous throughout, as well as by the spirit, vivacity, and good sense of the general narrative." *Quarterly Review.*

"To every species of readers, these volumes will prove a most entertaining repast; but to the scholar a *bonne bouche.*" *Brit. Crit. June,* 1815.

RECOLLECTIONS of ITALY, ENGLAND and AMERICA, with Essays on various subjects in Morals and Literature.
By F. A. DE CHATEAUBRIAND,
Author of "Travels in Greece and Palestine," "Beauties of Christianity," &c. &c. In 8vo. price 225 cents, in boards.

"M. Chateaubriand's Recollections are full of the same fire and beauty that pervade his more finished performances." *Lit. Pan.*

"We recognize in these recollections the elegant and romantic author of Atala; his fervid imagination and vivid descriptions. These recollections abound in sublime descriptions, picturesque imagery, and noble thoughts." *Literary Register.*

A VOYAGE TO THE DEMERARY, containing a statistical account of the settlements there, and of those on the Essequibo, the Berbice, and other contiguous Rivers of Guyana. By HENRY BOLINGBROKE, Esq.
In 8vo. Price 150 cents in boards.

A

VOYAGES AND TRAVELS to Brazil, the South Sea, Kamschatka, Japan, the Aleutian Islands, the North-West Coast of America, and the North-East part of Asia, through Siberia to St. Petersburgh, during the years 1803, 4, 5, 6, and 7. By G. V. LANGSDORFF, Aulic Counsellor to His Majesty the Emperor of Russia, Consul General at the Brazils, &c. &c. Price 3 dollars in boards.

In one large volume 8vo. with a Frontispiece.

"The account of the Russian Embassy to Japan, which this celebrated naturalist has here given to the public, possesses great claims on their attention, his principal aim having been to compile a popular narrative, in which he has described the most interesting objects, the manners and customs of the nations visited, their modes of living, the productions of the countries, &c. &c." *Mon. Mag.*

TRAVELS OF ALI BEY, IN MOROCCO, TRIPOLI, CYPRUS, EGYPT, ARABIA, SYRIA, AND TURKEY, between the years 803 and 1807. Written by himself, and translated into English. In 2 vols. 8vo. with a Map of the Northern Part of Africa, and eight other engravings.

Price 5 dollars 50 cents in boards.

*** Ali Bey has been long known to men of science in various parts of Europe. Travelling as a Mussulman and Prince, he has been enabled to give, among much curious matter, some new and interesting relations, which no Christian has ever had the opportunity of doing. He had the privilege of visiting the Temple of Mecca, and of washing and perfuming the Caaba, he most sacred office of the Mahometan religion. He has given a minute account of those ceremonies, and of the Weehabites, by whom he was taken prisoner, in his way to Medina: also, of the magnificent Temple built by the Mussulmen on the site of that of Solomon, and which no Christian has been suffered to inspect. He describes some curious Antiquities of Cythera, Idalia, and Paphos—and the Temple or Mosque of Job, in Constantinople, where the Sultan, at his accession, is girt with the sabre, and into which no Christian has been able to penetrate. The substance of these Travels has been read before the National Institute at Paris, and excited great interest there.

LETTERS ON ENGLAND: Comprising descriptive scenes; with remarks on the state of society, domestic economy, habits of the people, and condition of the manufacturing classes generally. Interspersed with miscellaneous observations and reflections.

By JOSHUA E. WHITE, of Savannah.

In 2 vols. 8vo. Price 450 cents in boards.

SCRIPTURE ATLAS, containing 10 4to. Maps, viz. 1. Journeyings of the Children of Israel from Rameses to the Land of Promise; 2. Map of Canaan as promised to Abraham and his posterity; 3. Map of Egypt; 4. Map of the places recorded in the five Books of Moses; 5. Map of Canaan in the time of Joshua; 6. Map of the purveyorships in the Reign of Solomon; 7. Syria and Assyria; 8. Map of the Dominions of Solomon; 9. Map of the Land of Moriah, or Jerusalem and the adjacent country; 10. Map of the Travels of the Apostles. Price 150 cents half bound.

AN ACCOUNT of a VOYAGE to ABYSSINIA, and TRAVELS in the **INTERIOR** of that **COUNTRY,** executed under the orders of the British government, in the years 1809 and 1810; in which are included an account of the **PORTUGUESE SETTLEMENTS** on the **EASTERN COAST of AFRICA,** visited in the course of the voyage; a concise summary of late occurrences in Arabia Felix; and some particulars respecting the Aboriginal African Tribes, extending from Mozambique to the borders of Egypt, together with vocabularies of their respective languages.

By HENRY SALT, Esq. F. R. S. &c.

In 1 vol. 8vo. with a Map of Abyssinia.

Price 275 cents in boards.

(3)

VOYAGES, TRAVELS, GEOGRAPHY, &c.

PERSONAL NARRATIVE of Travels to the EQUINOCTIAL REGIONS of the NEW CONTINENT between the years 1799—1804. By ALEXANDER DE HUMBOLDT, and AIME BONPLAND. Written in French, By ALEXANDER DE HUMBOLDT.
And translated into English by HELEN MARIA WILLIAMS.
In 8vo. Price 250 cents in Boards.

TRAVELS in the INTERIOR of BRAZIL; preceded by an account of a voyage to the Rio de la Plata. By JOHN MAWE, Author of a Treatise on the Mineralogy of Derbyshire. In 1 vol. 8vo. illustrated with plates, and a map. Price 3 dollars in boards.

CAREY'S GENERAL ATLAS, improved. Being a collection of MAPS of the WORLD and QUARTERS, their Kingdoms, States, &c. containing fifty-eight Maps, handsomely coloured. 1. The World; 2. ditto. Mercator's projection; 3. North America; 4. The British Possessions in America; 5. The United States; 6. Vermont; 7. New-Hampshire; 8. Maine; 9. Massachusetts; 10. Rhode-Island; 11. Connecticut; 12. New-York; 13. New-Jersey; 14. Pennsylvania; 15. Delaware; 16. Maryland; 17. Virginia; 18. North-Carolina; 19. South-Carolina; 20. Georgia; 21. Kentucky; 22. Tennessee; 23. The Mississippi Territory; 24. Ohio; 25. The North Western, Michigan, Illinois, and Indiana Territories; 26. The State of Louisiana; 27. The Missouri Territory; 28. Seven Ranges of Townships laid out by Congress; 29. Mexico; 30. The West Indies; 31. The French part of St. Domingo; 32. South America; 33. Caracas; 34. Peru; 35. Chili and the vice-royalty of La Plata; 36. Brazil; 37. Europe; 38. Sweden, Denmark, and Norway; 39. Russia; 40. Scotland; 41. England and Wales; 42. Ireland; 43. United Provinces and Netherlands; 44. Germany; 45. France, divided into Departments; 46. Hungary and Turkey in Europe; 47. Spain and Portugal; 48. Italy; 49. Switzerland; 50. Poland; 51. Asia; 52. China; 53. Hindostan; 54. Islands and Channels between China and New Holland; 55. New South Wales, with Norfolk Island, Lord Howe's Island, Port Jackson, &c.; 56. Africa; 57. Countries round the North Pole; 58. Captain Cook's Discoveries.
In folio. Price 15 dollars, handsomely half bound.

SKETCHES, HISTORICAL and DESCRIPTIVE, of LOUISIANA.
By Major AMOS STODDARD, Member of the U. S. M. P. S.
and of the New York Historical Society.
In 8vo. Price 3 dollars, in boards.

"This volume is divided into fourteen chapters, comprehending the history of Louisiana and the Floridas; their geography, government, laws, commerce, and manufactures, learning and religion. The character of the Louisianians, the state of slavery amongst them, the antiquities, the rivers, and mineral riches of that country; a description of the aborigines, and the arguments in favour of the conjecture that this country was settled by emigration from Wales, anterior to the discovery of Columbus, conclude the volume.

"The style, although it assumes the character of humble narrative, is pure and chaste, and we cordially congratulate the author on the hardihood of character he has assumed, for such undoubtedly it is, in the present day, to be so unclassical as to write common sense. He shows himself to be a master of the materials that he manages, and, while conversing with his page, we have found ourselves seated with him by the side of solitary rivers, plunging into the glooms of inextricable wildernesses, or climbing the heights of desert mountains, instead of forgetting all these and admiring the brilliancy of a paragraph. We wished to explore the regions of Louisiana: and by the light of his lamp we have explored them." *Port Folio.*

ATLAS MINIMUS, or a new set of POCKET MAPS of various EMPIRES, KINGDOMS, and STATES, with Geographical extracts relative to each. Drawn and Engraved by J. GIBSON.
In 18mo. Price 1 dollar, half bound.

CAREY'S AMERICAN POCKET ATLAS, containing 23 Maps, viz. 1. United States; 2. Vermont; 3. New-Hampshire; 4. Maine; 5. Massachusetts; 6. Rhode-Island; 7. Connecticut; 8. New-York; 9. New-Jersey; 10. Pennsylvania; 11. Delaware; 12. Ohio; 13. Maryland; 14. Virginia; 15. Kentucky; 16. North-Carolina; 17. Tennessee; 18. South-Carolina; 19. Georgia; 20. Mississippi Territory; 21. Upper Territories of the United States; 22. Louisiana; 23. Missouri Territory. With a BRIEF DESCRIPTION of each STATE and TERRITORY. Also the Census of the Inhabitants of the United States for 1810, and the Exports for 20 years.
4th. edition, greatly improved and enlarged. Price 2 dollars, bound.

THE AMERICAN MINOR ATLAS; 4to. containing the same Maps as the preceding. Price 150 cents, half bound.

THE STRANGER'S GUIDE through PHILADELPHIA, containing a PLAN of the CITY, with an alphabetical list of all the Squares, Streets, Roads, Lanes, Alleys, Avenues, Courts, Ship-Yards, Public Buildings &c. in the City and Suburbs. By JOHN ADEMS PAXTON.
In 12mo. Price 150 cents, handsomely half bound.

TRAVELS THROUGH THE CANADAS, containing a description of the picturesque scenery of some of the Rivers and Lakes, with an account of the Productions, Commerce and Inhabitants of those Provinces.
BY GEORGE HERIOT, ESQ.
In 12mo. Price 1 dollar, in boards.
"Altogether we deem it one of the most curious publications that has of late appeared." *Monthly Mag.*

A JOURNEY through PERSIA, ARMENIA and ASIA MINOR, to CONSTANTINOPLE, in the years 1808 and 1809, in which is included some account of the proceedings of HIS MAJESTY'S MISSION under SIR HARFORD JONES, Bart. K. C. to the Court of the King of Persia.
By JAMES MORIER,
His Majesty's Secretary of Embassy to the Court of Persia.
In 1 vol. 8vo. with plates, and a Map.
Price 3 dollars in boards.

A GENERAL ATLAS, being a collection of MAPS of the WORLD and QUARTERS, their principal Empires, Kingdoms, &c. Containing 52 Maps and Charts, viz. 1. The World; 2. ditto Mercator's projection; 3. North America; 4. United States; 5. Eastern States, with part of Canada; 6. Middle and Western States; 7. Southern States; 8. North Western Territories; 9. Vermont; 10. New-Hampshire; 11. Maine; 12. Massachusetts; 13. Rhode-Island; 14. Connecticut; 15. New-York; 16. New-Jersey; 17. Pennsylvania; 18. Delaware; 19. Maryland; 20. Virginia; 21. North-Carolina; 22. South-Carolina; 23. Georgia; 24. Kentucky; 25. Tennessee; 26. Mississippi Territory; 27. Ohio; 28. Louisiana; 29. Missouri Territory; 30. West Indies; 31. South America; 32. Europe; 33. Russia, Northern Part; 34. Southern do; 35. Sweden, Denmark, Norway; 36. Poland; 37. Scotland; 38. England and Wales; 39. Ireland; 40. Netherlands; 41. United Provinces; 42. Germany; 43. France; 44. Switzerland; 45. Italy; 46. Spain and Portugal; 47. Turkey in Europe; 48. Asia; 49. Hindostan; 50. Turkey in Asia; 51. Islands between China and New Holland; 52. Africa. In 4to. Price 5 dollars, half bound.

SHEET MAPS of EUROPE, ASIA, AFRICA, and the Kingdoms into which they are divided.
Price 50 cents each, coloured.

(3)

SHEET MAPS of the **UNITED STATES**, and of all the **STATES** and **TERRITORIES**; **SOUTH AMERICA**, Brazil, Chili, Peru, Caracas, &c. Price 75 cents each, coloured.

The **TRAVELLER'S DIRECTORY**; or, **A POCKET COMPANION.** Shewing the course of the Main Road from Philadelphia to New York, and from Philadelphia to Washington, with descriptions of the places through which it passes, and the intersections of the cross roads. Illustrated with an account of such remarkable objects as are generally interesting to travellers. From actual survey. By S. S. MOORE and T. W. JONES.

Second Edition. In 8vo. Price 2 dollars, bound.

"The design and contents of this volume are fully expressed in the title page. The work is handsomely, and we believe, correctly executed. Every traveller on those roads will find it a useful and instructive companion. The plan of this directory is so judicious, that we hope the authors may find it for their interest to extend it to other parts of the United States.

Amer. Rev. and Lit. Jour.

HISTORY AND BIOGRAPHY.

MEMOIRS OF SIR JOSHUA REYNOLDS, Knt. late President of the Royal Academy, containing original Anecdotes of many distinguished persons, his contemporaries; and a brief Analysis of his discourses, to which are added, Varieties on Art.

By JAMES NORTHCOTE, R. A.

In 8vo. Price 3 dollars in boards.

"His professional merits and defects have been so ably and impartially discussed by his Biographer, in the general view of his works, that we have only to recommend it to the attentive perusal of every lover and practitioner of the Art.

"These discourses, we consider on the whole, as containing the soundest and best body of critical instruction that has ever been produced on the subject.

"We feel ourselves much indebted to Mr. Northcote for the work before us." *Edin. Rev.*

A SKETCH OF THE PUBLIC LIFE OF M. FOUCHE, Duke of Otranto; comprising various correspondence, addressed to the Emperor Napoleon, King Joachim, the Duke d'Artois, Prince Blucher, Louis XVIII, Count de Blacas, and other ministers, &c.

In 12mo. Price 75 cts. in boards.

"This work pourtrays this celebrated man as he really is. It exhibits his most secret sentiments, the spirit of his public life, and the principles which have directed him at all periods, and in situations the most diversified.

"This publication cannot fail to be read with avidity by all who take interest in the great events, and in the history of the most eminent characters of the present extraordinary age. *New Monthly Magazine.*

LIFE OF ANDREW JACKSON, Major General in the service of the United States: comprehending a History of the War in the South, from the commencement of the Creek campaign, to the termination of hostilities before New Orleans. Commenced by JOHN REID, Brevet Major U. S. A. Completed by JOHN HENRY EATON.

In 8vo. Price 4 dolls. bound.

MEMOIRS OF THE MARCHIONESS DE LAROCHE JAQUELEIN. In 8vo. With a Map of the Theatre of War in La Vendee.

Price 250 cents in boards.

"We think there are few recent productions of the French press likely to afford so much gratification to English readers." *Edinburgh Rev. Feb.* 1816.

HISTORY OF THE UNITED STATES, from the first settlement as English Colonies, in 1607, to the year 1808, or the thirty-third year of their Sovereignty and Independence. By DAVID RAMSAY, M. D. Continued to the Treaty of Ghent, by SAMUEL STANHOPE SMITH, D. D. L. L. D. and other literary gentlemen.

In 3 vols. 8vo. price 10 dollars, bound.

LIFE OF GEN. FRANCIS MARION, a celebrated Partizan Officer, in the Revolutionary War, in South Carolina and Georgia.

By the Rev. M. L. WEEMS,

Author of the "Life of Washington." Fourth edition, with engravings.

In 12mo. Price 1 dollar, bound.

THE LIFE OF DR. BENJAMIN FRANKLIN. Written chiefly by himself; with a collection of his Essays, humorous, moral, and literary. A new edition, revised and enlarged, By the Rev. M. L. WEEMS, Author of "Life of Marion," and "Life of Washington."

In 12mo. Price1 dollar, bound.

DR. RUSSEL'S HISTORY OF MODERN EUROPE, continued down to the Treaty of Amiens in 1802.

By CHARLES COOTE, L. L. D.

The large annual impressions, which for more than thirty years were called for to supply the demand for this excellent Work in England, may be considered conclusive evidence of its merits in the public estimation. During the author's life time, each succeeding edition was improved by himself:—he lived to make it a perfect Compendium of Modern History, and has left it an honourable monument of his fame and talents.

This work contains A Brief View of the Decline and Fall of the Roman Empire. The Rise of Modern Kingdoms generally. A particular History of the French Monarchy. A particular History of Spain from the Dominion of the Visigoths. Italy, with the rise and progress of the Temporal power of the Popes. Britain—from its relinquishment by the Romans. Ireland. The German Empire—from Charlemagne. The Empire of Constantinople—till its overthrow. Empire of the Arabs. Rise and progress of the Turks, and fall of the Greek Empire. History of Portugal. View of the Progress of Navigation. Conquests in the East and West Indies. Discovery of America, &c. History of Sweden, Denmark, Norway, Russia, Poland, and Prussia. North America—as connected with European History. The rise, progress, and termination of the Revolutionary War of this Country. The progress and immense aggrandizement of the British power in India. The Wars of the French Revolution till the Treaty of Amiens. A very comprehensive and highly useful Chronology.

Third American edition. In 5 vols. 8vo. Price 15 dollars, Bound.

AMERICAN CHRONOLOGY, from the DISCOVERY of the WESTERN WORLD till May, 1813. By THOMAS CLARK, Author of Naval History of the United States. In 24mo. Price 25 cents, in boards.

MEMOIRS, &c. of GENERAL MOREAU, with a fac-simile of his last letter to his wife, and an engraved plan of the passage of the Rhine at Strasbourg. By JOHN PHILIPPART, Esq. author of "Memoirs of Bernadotte," &c. &c. In 8vo. Price 2 dollars, in boards.

"Every event, connected with the public and private life of General Moreau, the author has drawn together, and embodied with the utmost fidelity and circumspection." *Eur. Mag. March,* 1814.

NAVAL HISTORY of the UNITED STATES, from the commencement of the REVOLUTIONARY WAR. By THOMAS CLARK.
2nd. edition. In 2 vols. 12mo. Price 2 dollars, in boards.

The DECLINE and FALL of the ROMAN EMPIRE.
By EDWARD GIBBON.
Second American Edition. In 8 volumes, 8vo.
Price 25 dollars bound.

MISCELLANEOUS.

AN EASY INTRODUCTION TO THE GAME OF CHESS; containing 100 Examples of Games, and a great variety of critical situations and conclusions; including the whole of Philidor's Analysis, with copious selections from Stamma, the Calabrois, &c. Arranged and made plain, with instructions for Learners; rendering a complete knowledge of the game perfectly easy of attainment.

CATECHISM OF POLITICAL ECONOMY; or, Familiar Conversations on the manner in which Wealth is produced, distributed and consumed in society. By JEAN BAPTISTE SAY, author of a Treatise on Political Economy. Translated from the French, by JOHN RICHTER.
In 8vo. Price 1 dollar, in boards.

This work contains truths, which it would well become politicians to consider and meditate with earnestness. *Lit. Pan.*

Of this work, the Monthly Magazine says,—" A more acceptable service could not well be rendered the country, than by publishing this valuable elementary treatise."

ENCYCLOPÆDIA OF WIT. A Choice Collection of Anecdotes, Jests, Bon-mots, &c. &c. from the latest British Publications.
In 18mo. Price 63 cents, bound.

ELEMENTS OF CRITICISM. By HENRY HOME, of Kames.
In 2 vols. 8vo. Price 550 cents, bound.

PARIS CHIT CHAT; or a View of the Society, Manners, Customs, Literature and Amusements of the Parisians. Being a translation of " Guillaume, Le Franc Parleur," and a sequel to the " Paris Spectator."
In 2 vols. 18mo. Price 175 cents in boards.

THE PARIS SPECTATOR; or, L'HERMITE DE LA CHAUSSEE D'ANTIN. Containing Observations upon PARISIAN MANNERS and CUSTOMS at the Commencement of the Nineteenth Century. Translated from the French, By WILLIAM JERDAN.
In 3 vols. 18mo. Price 225 cents. in Boards.

THE COLONIAL POLICY OF GREAT BRITAIN, considered with relation to her NORTH AMERICAN PROVINCES, and West India Possessions; wherein the DANGEROUS TENDENCY of AMERICAN COMPETITION is attempted to be developed, and the necessity of re-commencing a Colonial System on a vigorous and extensive scale, exhibited and defended: with plans for the promotion of Emigration, and STRICTURES on the TREATY of GHENT.
By a British Traveller.
In 12mo. Price one dollar in boards.

*** The alarming views of the relations, present and future, between the United States and Great Britain, which are developed in this work, have impressed the American publisher with the idea that it could not fail to be useful to re-print and disseminate it here. It merits the most serious attention of the legislators and politicians of this nation. Should the policy it advocates be unfortunately adopted by Great Britain, there will be an imperious necessity for measures of counteraction.

PRINTED FOR M. CAREY & SON, PHILADELPHIA.

RULES AND REGULATIONS for the SWORD EXERCISE of the CAVALRY. By JOHN HEWES.
With 28 plates. In 8vo. Price 250 cents, bound.

An INQUIRY concerning the RISE and PROGRESS, the REDEMPTION and PRESENT STATE, and the MANAGEMENT of the NATIONAL DEBT of GREAT BRITAIN.
By ROBERT HAMILTON, L. L. D. F. R. S. E.
From the 2d London Edition.
In 8vo. Price 175 cents in boards.

"Dr. Hamilton has performed a most important service to his country, by directing the public attention to just views of this interesting subject.

"We have now stated the principal doctrines of this interesting publication. They are widely different from the opinions which have been hitherto prevalent, and which are sanctioned by the authority of great names: but they are supported by arguments which appear so convincing, and they lead to practical conclusions of such importance, that we trust they will be patiently and thoroughly canvassed; and we have no apprehension that the result will be unfavorable either to the author or his reviewer. While he condescends to instruct the young student in the first principles of this important subject, he opens views which deserve the attention of the most experienced statesman.
Edinburgh Review.

INSTRUCTIONS FOR THE DRILL, and the method of performing the Nineteen Manœuvres. By Lieut. JOHN RUSSELL.
With 33 plates. In 12mo. Price 125 cents, in boards.

AN ACADEMY FOR GROWN HORSEMEN. Containing the completest Instructions for Walking, Trotting, Cantering, Galloping, Stumbling, and Tumbling. By GEOFFREY GAMBADO, Esq.
Riding Master, Master of the Horse, and Grand Equerry to the Doge of Venice.
Embellished with 12 Caricatures, from designs by Bunbury. In 12mo. Price 75 cents, in boards.

"To turn and wind a fiery Pegasus,
"And witch the world with noble Horsemanship."

"With great delight do we hail this satisfactory republication of a work originally published before our critical existence, but always the source of hearty merriment and gratification to us. The singular and truly original humour of the writing, and the unrivalled burlesque of the plates, have always made these books prime favourites, with all who had any relish for harmless wit and satire, by which no individual is hurt. *Brit. Crit.*

THE OLIVE BRANCH; or, FAULTS ON BOTH SIDES, FEDERAL and DEMOCRATIC. A serious Appeal on the Necessity of mutual Forgiveness and Harmony. By M. CAREY.
Eighth edition, enlarged. In 8vo. Price 3 dolls. handsomely bound.

THE CRIMINAL RECORDER; or, an AWFUL BEACON to the RISING GENERATION of both Sexes, erected by the arm of Justice to persuade them from the dreadful Miseries of Guilt. Collected from authentic documents, By A FRIEND OF MAN. With 6 Engravings.
In 12mo. Price 1 dollar, bound.

THE HOUSE CARPENTER'S BOOK of PRICES, and Rules for Measuring and Valuing all their different kinds of work.
In 12mo. Price 75 cents, half bound.

THE IMMORTAL MENTOR; or, MAN'S UNERRING GUIDE to a Healthy, Wealthy and Happy life. In 3 parts.
By LEWIS CORNARO, Dr. FRANKLIN, and Dr. SCOTT.

The CONGRESS OF VIENNA. By the ABBE DE PRADT, author of the "History of the Mission to Warsaw," &c. &c. Translated from the French.

In 8vo. Price 150 cents in boards.

* * To those who would look into futurity, and see the probable results of the Congress of Vienna, the recent work of M. De Pradt will be an acceptable wand. It will enable the inquisitive politician to judge, with some reasonable accuracy, whether the present condition of Europe be settled, on a peace, or a war establishment.

THE AMERICAN MISCELLANY. Prose and verse. Original and Selected. In 2 vols. 12mo. Price 2 dollars, bound.

A SENTIMENTAL JOURNEY through France and Italy.
By LAWRENCE STERNE.
With 6 Engravings. In 18mo. Price 63 cents, bound.

FARRIERY IMPROVED; or, a complete Treatise on the ART OF FARRIERY. Wherein are fully explained the Nature and Structure of that useful creature, a Horse; with the Diseases and accidents he is liable to; and the methods of cure. Exemplified by 10 elegant cuts, each the full figure of a Horse. Describing all the various parts of that noble animal. By HENRY BRACKEN, M. D.
In 18mo. Price 50 cents, half bound.

REGULATIONS for the ORDER and DISCIPLINE of the TROOPS of the UNITED STATES. By BARON STEUBEN.
With plates. Price 50 cents, half bound.

VOYAGES to LILLIPUT and BROBDIGNAG.
By LEMUEL GULLIVER.
In 18mo. with plates. Price 63 cents, half bound.

THE MORAL MIRROR; or, a LOOKING GLASS for Sots, Parasites, Gluttons, Clowns, Praters, Time-Servers, Pretenders, Knaves, Knights of the post, Atheists, Zealots, Hypocrites, &c. &c. selected from the "Characters," by BUTLER. Author of Hudibras. In 24mo. Price 50 cents, half bound.

LAW.

REPORTS OF CASES, argued and determined in the Court of King's Bench, with Tables of the Names of the Cases, and principal Matters. By EDWARD HYDE EAST, Esq. of the Inner Temple, Barrister at Law. A new edition, with corrections, and the addition of notes and references. By THOMAS DAY. In 16 vols. Royal 8vo. Price, bound in sheep, 72 dollars, or in calf, 80 dollars.

THE CLERKS' MAGAZINE and AMERICAN CONVEYANCERS' ASSISTANT; being a collection adapted to the United States, of the most approved Precedents of Affidavits, Agreements, Covenants, Assignments, Awards, Bargains and Sales, Bonds, &c. &c. containing nearly double the number of such Precedents, usually inserted in similar publications.
By HARRY TOULMIN, Secretary of the State of Kentucky.
In 12mo. Price 1 dollar, bound.

PRECEDENTS in the OFFICE of a JUSTICE of the PEACE.
By COLLINSON READ, Esq.
Foolscap 4to. Price 1 dollar, half bound.

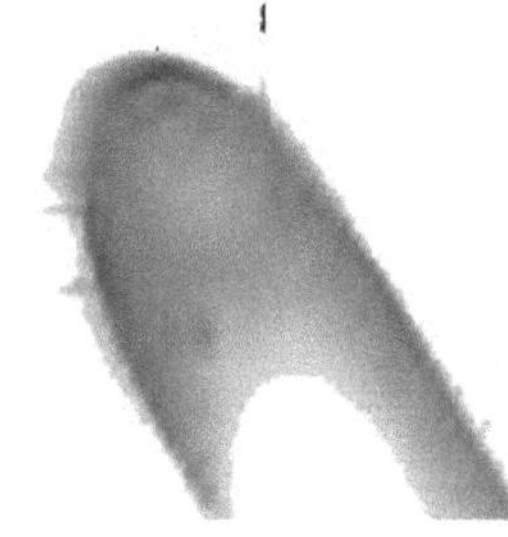

REPORTS OF CASES argued and adjudged in the Supreme Court of the United States. February Term, 1816.

By HENRY WHEATON,

Counsellor at Law. Vol. I. In 8vo. Price 7 dollars, bound in calf.

*** This volume contains, besides concise and faithful notes of the arguments of counsel, annotations on the cases reported, illustrating the decisions by analogous authorities, and the former decisions of the Supreme Court; and a copious Appendix, embracing a view of the Land Laws of Kentucky; of the Practical Prize Causes, and the Judicial History of the Rule of the War of 1756. It comprises a variety of Decisions in Chancery, Prize and Commercial Law—and the Local Laws of the different States of the Union, &c.

AN ESSAY ON AVERAGE, and other subjects connected with the contract of Marine Insurance.

By ROBERT STEVENS, of Lloyd's.

First American, from the 2d London edition. In 8vo. Price 250 cents, bound.

The high importance of the contents of this work to the particular branch of the community which it regards, induces us to point it out as a specimen of what may be accomplished by other writers, in different departments of mercantile business. *Monthly Rev. May*, 1817.

DIVINITY.

QUARTO BIBLES

No. *Coarse Paper, not lettered.*

No.		$
1.	Old and New Testaments,	3 75
2.	Old and New Testaments and Psalms	4 00
3.	Old and New Testaments and Apocrypha	4 25
4.	Old and New Testaments, Apocrypha and Psalms	4 50
	Coarse Paper, lettered and filleted.	
38.	Old and New Testaments, and Apocrypha	4 50
5.	Old and New Testaments, Apocrypha and 11 Plates,	5 00
6.	Old and New Testaments, Apocrypha and 25 Plates	5 50
7.	Old and New Testaments, Apocrypha, 11 Plates, and Psalms	5 25
15.	Old and New Testaments, Apocrypha and Concordance	5 25
16.	Old and New Testaments and Concordance	4 75
19.	Old and New Testaments, Apocrypha, Concordance, 25 Plates, and Ostervald's Notes	7 00
32.	Old and New Testaments, Apocrypha and Psalms	4 75
33.	Old and New Testaments, Apocrypha, Concordance, and 25 Plates,	6 25
	Common Paper filleted.	
48.	Old and New Testaments,	4 25
49.	Old and New Testaments and Apocrypha	4 75
	Common Paper, lettered and filleted.	
18.	Old and New Testaments,	4 50
17.	Old and New Testaments, Apocrypha, Concordance, 25 Maps and Plates	7 50
25.	Old and New Testaments, Apocrypha, Concordance, and 2 Maps	6 00
26.	Old and New Testaments and Apocrypha	5 00
27.	Old and New Testaments, Apocrypha, Concordance, and 10 Maps	7 00
34.	Old and New Testaments, Apocrypha, Concordance, 10 Maps, and Psalms	7 25
44.	Old and New Testaments, Apocrypha, and 11 Plates.	5 50
45.	Old and New Testaments, Apocrypha, 11 Plates and Psalms	5 75
46.	Old and New Testaments, Apocrypha, and 25 Plates	6 25
47.	Old and New Testaments, Apocrypha, 25 Plates and Psalms	6 50

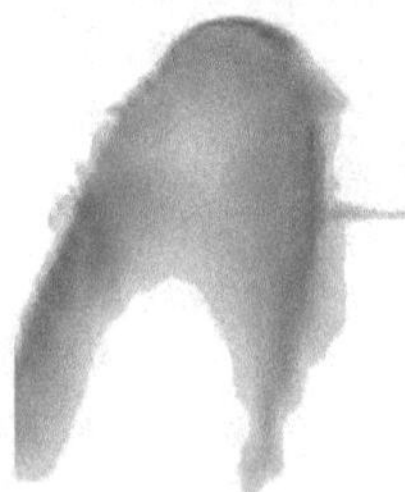

(3)

Fine Paper.

8.	Old and New Testaments,	6 00
9.	Old and New Testaments and Apocrypha	6 50
10.	Old and New Testaments, Apocrypha, Concordance & 2 Maps	7 50
11.	Old and New Testaments, Apocrypha, Concordance & 10 Maps	8 00
12.	Old and New Testaments, Apocrypha, Concordance & 25 Plates	8 50
13.	Old and New Testaments, Apocrypha, Concordance, 25 Plates and Psalms	8 75
14.	Old and New Testaments, Apocrypha, Concordance, 25 Maps and Plates, and Ostervald's Notes	9 50
28.	Old and New Testaments, Apocrypha, Concordance, 2 Maps, and Psalms	7 75
29.	Old and New Testaments, Apocrypha, and Psalms	6 75

Superfine Paper, bound in sheep.

21.	Old and New Testaments, Apocrypha, Concordance, 25 Plates & Psalms	10 25
20.	Old and New Testaments, Apocrypha, Concordance, 25 Maps and Plates, and Ostervald's Notes	11 00
22.	Old and New Testaments, Apocrypha, Concordance & 25 Plates	10 00
30.	Old and New Testaments, Apocrypha, Concordance, & 10 Maps	9 25
31.	Old and New Testaments, Apocrypha, Concordance, 10 Maps and Psalms	9 50
35.	Old and New Testaments, and Apocrypha	8 00
40.	Old and New Testaments, Apocrypha, Concordance & 70 Plates	12 50
50.	Old and New Testaments, Apocrypha, Concordance & 100 Plates	16 00

Superfine Paper, bound in Calf or Morocco.

23.	Old and New Testaments, Apocrypha, Concor. and 25 plates, plain calf	11 50
24.	Old and New Testaments, do. do. do. do. Morocco, gilt	13 00
39.	Old and New Testaments, do. do. do. do. calf extra	13 00
41.	Old and New Testaments, Apocrypha, Concordance, & 70 plates, Morocco gilt	15 00
42.	Old and New Testaments, do. do. do. do. calf extra	15 00
43.	Old and New Testaments, do. do. do. do. do. gilt edges	18 00
51.	Old and New Testaments, do. do. and 100 Plates, calf,	17 00
52.	Old and New Testaments, do. do. do. do. calf extra,	18 00
53.	Old and New Testaments, do. do. do. do. Morocco, gilt,	18 00
54.	Old and New Testaments, do. do. do. do. do. & gilt edges,	20 00

SCHOOL BIBLES 12mo. *Coarse Paper.*	1 00
——— per doz.	9 00
——— with Psalms	1 13
——— per doz.	9 50
——— Fine paper, *lettered*	1 25
TESTAMENTS. *Coarse paper.*	38
——— per doz.	3 50
——— Fine paper	50

SERMONS, by the late WALTER BLAKE KIRWAN, Dean of Killala. With a sketch of his Life. In 8vo. Price 175 cents, boards.

"Dr. Kirwan called forth the latent virtues of the human heart, and taught men to discover in themselves a mine of charity, of which the proprietors had been unconscious. He came to interrupt the repose of the pulpit, and shakes one world with the thunder of the other. The preacher's desk becomes the throne of light." *Mr. Grattan's Speech, June 19, 1792*

"Mr Kirwan's powers of eloquence exceed any previous examples which are to be found in our language." *Monthly Review.*

The SECOND JOURNAL of the Stated Preacher to the Hospital and Alms-house in the City of New York, for a part of the year of our Lord, 1813. With an appendix. In 12mo. Price 1 dollar, in boards.

"Benevolence from its nature, composes the mind, warms the heart, enlivens the whole frame, and lightens every feature of the countenance."
Dr. Reid.

"This Journal is continued only half a year, but in the same style of pious simplicity as the former volume. The appendix is rendered highly interesting, by its containing the history of an actress and the sequel to the remarkable story of the mysterious Caroline, contained in the former Journal, and which its readers cannot have forgotten. The volume is, however, on the whole, calculated to excite strong interest in the minds of the friends of religion and humanity. *Eclectic Review, July 1816.*

SERMONS TO YOUNG WOMEN. 2 vols. in one.
By JAMES FORDYCE, D. D.
In 12mo. Price, 1 dollar, bound.

L'ANGE CONDUCTEUR dans la devotion chretienne, reduite en pratique en faveur des Ames Devotes; Par JAQUES GORET.
In 18mo. Price 113 cents, bound.

The GARDEN OF THE SOUL; or, a manual of Spiritual Exercises and instructions for Christians, who living in the world, aspire to devotion. To which is added, Vespers for Sundays.
By RICHARD CHALLENOR, D. D.
4th American edition, improved. 18mo. Price on common paper, 75 cents; on fine paper, lettered, 1 dollar.

The VADE MECUM; or, Manual of select and necessary devotions. In 32mo. Price on coarse paper, 38 cents; on fine paper, with cuts, lettered, 63 cents.

JOURNEE DU CHRETIEN, Sanctifiee par la priere et la Meditation. Nouvelle edition, en Latin et en François augmentee de plusieres prieres.
In 18mo. Price 75 cents, bound.

NINE SERMONS, on the Nature of the Evidence by which the fact of our Lord's Resurrection is established; and on various other subjects. To which is prefixed, a Dissertation on the Prophecies of the Messiah dispersed among the Heathen.

By SAMUEL HORSLEY, L.L.D. F.R.S. F.A.S. Late Lord Bishop of St. Asaph. In 8vo. Price 150 cents in boards.

"Every fragment of this prelate is precious; and though posthumous works in general require much indulgence, none of the writings of Bishop Horsley can fail to give delight to those who have a relish for original arguments on important subjects. *Analectic Mag.*

An ABRIDGMENT of the CHRISTIAN DOCTRINE,
By BISHOP HAY. In 18mo. Price 31 cents, bound.

THINK WELL ON'T; or, reflections on the Great Truths of the Christian Religion. For every day in the month.
By RICHARD CHALLENOR, D. D.
34th edition, In 18mo. Price 31 cents, bound.

The PIOUS CHRISTIAN INSTRUCTED, in the nature and practice of the principal exercises of Piety used in the Catholic Church.
By BISHOP HAY.
In 12mo. Price, 1 dollar, bound.

PETITES ETRENNES SPIRITUELLES, Contenant les prieres et offices, et la Messe, Latin—François. A L'usage universel.
In 32mo. with cuts, Price 44 cents, bound.

(3)

The DOWAY TESTAMENT. In 4to. with 11 plates. Price, 4 dollars, bound.

EXERCICIO QUOTIDIANO, Oraciones y devotiones para antes y despues de la Confesion, y Sagrada Comunion.
In 24mo. Price 63 cents, bound.

MEDICINE, SURGERY AND CHEMISTRY.

AN ESSAY ON PUERPERAL FEVER, illustrated by Cases which occurred in Leeds and its vicinity, in the years 1809—1812. By WILLIAM HEY. In 8vo. Price 150 cents in boards.

Whatever may be the general inference upon this subject, this little treatise will be deemed a perspicuous and judicious history of a severe and dangerous epidemic, and characterized by a sound pathological knowledge, clear arrangement, and great correctness of composition; and worthy to be classed with the best monographs of modern medical literature.
Edinburgh Medical and Surgical Journal, Oct. 1815.

VEGETABLE MATERIA MEDICA OF THE U. STATES; or, MEDICAL BOTANY: Containing a Botanical, General, and Medical History of Medicinal Plants, indigenous to the United States; illustrated by coloured Engravings, made after Original Drawings from Nature, done by the Author. By WILLIAM P. C. BARTON, M. D. Surgeon in the Navy of the United States, and of the Hospital for Marines at the Navy Yard, Philadelphia; Fellow of the College of Physicians, of Philadelphia, Member of the American Philosophical Society; President of the Philadelphia Linnæan Society; and Professor of Botany in the University of Pennsylvania.

No. 1, in 4to. Price 3 dollars. The succeeding numbers will appear every two months until the completion of the work, which will be in 8 numbers.

LECTURES ON INFLAMMATION, exhibiting a view of the general doctrines, Pathological and Practical, of Medical Surgery.
By JOHN THOMSON, M. D. F. R. S. E.
In 8vo. Price 3 dollars in boards.

A PRACTICAL ESSAY on Chemical Re-agents, or Tests, illustrated by a series of Experiments.
By FREDRICK ACCUM, Operative Chemist.
In 12mo. Price 1 dollar in boards.

"This little work will be found of considerable utility to the chemical student." *Thompson's Annals of Philosophy.*

A TREATISE ON FRACTURES, LUXATIONS, and other Affections of the Bones. By P. I. DESAULT. Translated by CHARLES CALDWELL, M. D. Third edition. In 8vo. Price 275 cents, bound.

ESSAYS ON HYPOCHONDRICAL AND OTHER NERVOUS AFFECTIONS. By JOHN REID, M. D. Member of the Royal College of Physicians, London, &c. &c. In 8vo. Price 150 cents in boards.

"The reader of these Essays will not have turned many pages of the book over, before he perceives that he is engaged with no ordinary writer."
Eclectic Review, August, 1816.

LECTURES ON THE ELEMENTS OF CHEMISTRY, delivered in the University of Edinburgh. By the late JOHN BLACK, M. D. Professor of Chemistry in that University, Physician to his Majesty, for Scotland, &c. &c. Published from his manuscripts, by JOHN ROBINSON, L. L. D. Professor of Natural Philosophy in the University of Edinburgh. In 3 vols. 8vo. with plates. Price 8 dollars, bound.

THE STUDENTS' CHEMICAL POCKET COMPANION.
By WILLIAM S. JACOBS, M. D.
In 12mo. Price 88 cents, bound.

A DICTIONARY OF PRACTICAL SURGERY, containing a complete exhibition of the present state of the PRINCIPLES and PRACTICE OF SURGERY, collected from the best and most original sources of information, and illustrated by Critical Remarks, By SAMUEL COOPER, Member of the Royal College of Surgeons, and author of the "First Lines of the Practice of Surgery." With notes and additions,
By JOHN SYNG DORSEY, M. D.
Adjunct professor of Surgery in the University of Pennsylvania.
Second American edition. In 2 vols.8vo. Price 7 dollars, bound.

MEDICAL INQUIRIES and OBSERVATIONS,
By BENJAMIN RUSH, M. D.
4th edition, In 2 vols. 8vo. Price 6 dollars, bound.

POETRY.

THE POETIC MIRROR, or, the Living Bards of Britain,
In 18mo. Price 75 cents, boards.

Containing the Guerilla—Lord Byron:—Epistle to R. S——; and Wat a' the Cleuch—Walter Scott; the Stranger; the Flying Taylor; and James Rigg—W. Wordsworth: the Gude Greye Katt—James Hogg: Isabelle; and the Cherub—S. T. Coleridge: Peter of Barnet; the Curse of the Laureate; and Carmen Judicisle—R. Southey; the Morning Star, or the Steam-Boat of Alloa; Hymn to the Moon; and the Stranded Ship—J. Wilson.

"Here is a thing as good as the Rejected Addresses with less broad comedy, but more of chastened humour; a thing which at once gives evidence of a fine faculty of distinguishing the poetical character of the authors imitated, and the greatest powers of touch in the delineation of their style."
Augustan Rev. Dec. 1816.

The MISSIONARY; a Poem. By W. L. BOWLES.
In 18mo. Price 75 cents, in Boards.

"Absolutely, this is one of the sweetest little poems that we remember to have lately perused." *Crit. Rev. Aug.* 1815.

CHILDE ALARIQUE, or, A POET'S REVERIE. In 24mo. Price 38 cents, in boards.

FABLES FOR THE LADIES. By EDWARD MOORE. To which are added, seven select fables, by other authors. In 18mo. Price 38 cents.

POEMS; original and translated. By RICHARD DABNEY. In 24mo. Price 63 cents, in boards.

"It possesses real merit, and will experience, as we flatter ourselves, a reception from the public different from that which usually awaits the productions of the American muse. It is a pleasing little morsel, skilfully prepared by the hand of genius, and delicately seasoned by learning and taste, and will not fail to gratify the palates of those whose chief delight is in the "feast of the mind." *Port Folio, July,* 1815.

THE PARNASSIAN GARLAND, or BEAUTIES of MODERN POETRY; consisting of upwards of two hundred pieces, selected from the works of the most distinguished Poets of the present age. With introductory lines to each article. Designed for the use of schools, and the admirers of poetry in general. By JOHN EVANS, A. M. In 18mo. Price 88 cents in boards.

THE HIGHLANDERS, and other POEMS. By Mrs. GRANT of Laggan. In 18mo. Price 50 cents, in boards.

"There is a strain of simplicity and unaffected feeling in these poems, which will give them a permanent interest. They are much to be recommended." *Month. Mag.*

(3)

THE FOREST MINSTREL. By JAMES HOGG, Author of "The Queen's Wake," "Pilgrims of the Sun," &c. &c. In 18mo. Price 88 cents, boards.

MARGARET OF ANJOU. A Poem. By MISS HOLFORD, Author of "Wallace; or, the Fight of Falkirk." In 18mo. Price 1 dollar, boards.

YOUNG'S POETICAL WORKS, Complete. With plates. In 2 vols. 24mo. Price 2 dollars, in boards.

CABINET OF MOMUS; a choice selection of HUMOUROUS POEMS, from Pindar, Dibdin, Colman, Freneau, Penrose, Hopkinson, Ladd, Humphreys, Harrison, Swift, Taylor, Pitt, &c. &c. Embellished with 6 engravings. In 12mo. Price 80 cents, bound.

YOUNG'S NIGHT THOUGHTS. In 24mo. with plates. Price 1 dollar, in boards.

EMILIA OF LINDINAU; or, the FIELD OF LEIPSIC. A Poem, in four cantos.

By MARY ARNALD HOUGHTON.

The DANCE of DEATH, and other Poems. By WALTER SCOTT, q. In 24mo. Price 38 cents in boards.

BALLAD ROMANCES, and other POEMS.
By Miss ANNA MARIA PORTER,
Author of "Recluse of Norway," Hungarian Brothers," &c. &c.
In 18mo. price 75 cents in boards.

"We are much mistaken if Miss Porter's Readers do not agree with us, in commending her muse." *Eur. Mag.*

"This very pleasing little volume is strongly recommended by the easy simplicity of its verses, and their perfectly moral tendency. *Gen. Mag.*

THE PASTORAL; or, LYRIC MUSE OF SCOTLAND. A Poem by HECTOR MACNEILL, Esq. 24mo. Price 38 cents, in boards.

MASONIC SONG BOOK, containing a large Collection of the most approved Masonic Songs, Odes, Anthems, &c. With 3 engravings. In 12mo. Price 88 cents, in boards

TALES OF TERROR. With 3 Caricature plates. In 12mo. Price 88 cents, in boards.

"This is really a happy piece of humour." *Brit. Crit.*

MINSTRELSY of the SCOTTISH BORDER; consisting of Historical and Romantic Ballads, collected in the Southern Counties of Scotland, with a few of Modern Date founded upon local tradition.
By WALTER SCOTT, Esq.
In 24mo. Price 1 dollar, in boards.

NOVELS, &c.

MATILDA; or, THE BARBADOES GIRL. A Tale. By MRS. HOFLAND, author of "Son of a Genius," "Maid of Moscow," &c. &c.
In 18mo. Price 63 cents, in boards.

ADOLPHE. A Novel. By M. BENJAMIN DE CONSTANT.
In 12mo. Price one dollar, in boards.

The style of this work is at once elevated and simple, and as an observer of human nature, in its most polished form of society and manners, as well as in its wildest extravagance of passion, M. de Constant yields neither to Rochefaucault, nor to M. Bruyere."

Augustan Rev. Nov. 1816.

PATIENCE AND PERSEVERANCE; or the MODERN GRISELDA. A Novel in 2 vols. By Mrs. HOFLAND, Author of "Maid of Moscow," "Son of a Genius," &c. &c. Price 2 dollars, in boards.

THE WARD OF DELAMERE. A Novel in 2 vols. By Mrs. PINCHARD. Price 2 dollars in boards.

LORIMER. A Tale. By LUCY AIKIN. In 12mo. Price 1 dollar in boards.

"Though the general character under which we class the work before us, be not eminently our favourite, it is here carried to such high excellence that it is impossible for us to withhold our approbation.

The story excites an uncommonly powerful interest in the reader's mind, and promotes the cause of morality and prudence by exhibiting the consequences of unrestrained rashness and passion." *Crit. Rev.*

THE YOUNG MOTHER; or ALBINIA. A Novel. By the author of "Rosa in London," &c. &c. In 12mo. Price 1 dollar; in boards.

FATHER AS HE SHOULD BE; a Novel in 2 vols. By Mrs HOFLAND, Author of "Maid of Moscow," "Son of a Genius," &c. &c. Price 2 dollars, in boards.

"Most of the characters are well imagined; the moral is good, and the tale a lesson for married men in their grand climacteric, who are not absolutely incorrigible." *Crit. Rev. July*, 1815.

THE HEART AND THE FANCY; or VALSINORE. A Tale. By Miss BENGER. In 12mo. Price 1 dollar, in boards.

PAIRED—NOT MATCHED; or MATRIMONY IN THE 19th CENTURY. By Mrs. ROSS. In 2 vols. 12mo. Price 2 dollars, in boards.

"We recommend this novel to our newly married fashionables." *Critical Review.*

TRECOTHICK BOWER; or LADY OF THE WEST COUNTRY. A Tale in 2 vols. By REGINA MARIA ROCHE, Author of the "Children of the Abbey," &c. &c. Price 2 dollars, in boards.

THE MAGIC OF WEALTH. A Novel. By T. S. SURR, Author of "A Winter in London," &c. &c. In 2 vols. 12mo. Price 2 dollars, in boards.

"There is much insight into character, with a very fair share of humour. *Brit. Crit. July*, 1815.

TRAITS OF NATURE. A Novel. By Miss. BURNEY. In 2 vols. Price 225 cents, in boards.

"A fertile invention, a dexterity of management, and a fluency of style, are manifest in these volumes." *Mon. Rev. Vol.* 71.

MARRIED LIFE; or FAULTS ON ALL SIDES. By Miss HOWARD. In 2 vols. 18mo. Price 2 dollars, in boards. Second American edition.

VATHEK. Translated from the Original French. With Notes. From the third London edition, revised and corrected. In 18mo. Price 88 cents, boards.

MORNTON. A novel, By Miss CULLEN, Author of "Home." In 3 vols. 12mo. Price 3 dollars

GERALDINE FAUCONBERG. A Novel in 2 vols.
By Miss BURNEY, Author of "Traits of Nature," "Tales of Fancy," &c. &c.

EMMA. A Novel. By the author of "Sense and Sensibility," "Pride and Prejudice," &c.

"The work before us proclaims a knowledge of the human heart, with the power and resolution to bring that knowledge to the service of honour and virtue. Keeping close to common incidents, and to such characters as occupy the ordinary walks of life, she has produced sketches of such spirit and originality, that we never miss the excitation which depends upon a narrative of uncommon events, arising from the consideration of minds, manners, and sentiments, greatly above our own." *Quarterly Review.*

DISCIPLINE. By the author of "Self Controul." In 2 vols. 12mo. 2d. American edition. Price 2 dollars, bound.

"These volumes have almost every merit that can recommend fictitious writing—interest of narrative—happy delineation of characters—vivid description of scenery and of manners, and purity and elegance of style."
Ana. Mag. Sept. 1815.

ROSA IN LONDON. In 18mo. Price 63 cents, in boards.

THE HUNGARIAN BROTHERS. By Miss ANNA MARIA PORTER. In 2 vols. 12mo. The 2d edition. Price 2 dollars, in boards.

"The incidents of this Novel are striking, and many of the characters are finely drawn. The two brothers are models of that chivalrous heroism with which Miss Porter has, on other occasions, proved herself to be intimately acquainted." *Crit. Rev.*

THE REFUSAL. By Mrs. WEST.
Author of "Tale of the Times." "Gossip's Story," &c. &c. In 2 vols. 12mo. Price 2 dollars, in boards.

THE HAWTHORN COTTAGE. A Tale. By J. JONES.
Two volumes in one. In 12mo. Price 1 dollar, in boards.

THE HISTORY OF TOM JONES, a Foundling.
By HENRY FIELDING, Esq.
In 3 vols. 18mo. Price 3 dollars, bound.

HOME. A Novel in 2 volumes. By Miss CULLEN, Daughter of the celebrated Dr. Cullen. Price 2 dollars in boards.

"Simple occurrences in elegant and chaste language, events which might take place in any family, form the ground-work of this pleasing Novel, in which there is much to commend, and nothing to blame." *Eur. Mag.*

THE LETTERS of an ITALIAN NUN and an ENGLISH GENTLEMAN. Supposed to be written by J. J. ROUSSEAU.
In 18mo. Price 50 cents, bound.

"Not Rousseau's—but in many respects worthy of his exquisite pen. The story is interesting and pathetic—and the letters are written with spirit and elegance." *Mon. Rev.*

ELIZABETH; or the EXILES OF SIBERIA. A Tale founded on fact. Translated from the French of MADAME COTTIN.
5th edition. In 18mo. Price 63 cents, bound.

"This charming little work is a translation from the French, and unlike most other translations, loses nothing of the spirit and interest contained in the original. *Lady's Museum.*

"We are not in general, particularly fond of novels founded on fact; but we must make an exception in favour of any thing so well executed as that which is now before us." *Edin. Rev.*

GULZARA, PRINCESS of PERSIA; or, the VIRGIN QUEEN. A Satirical Novel.

In 12mo. Price one dollar in boards.

This Edition is provided with a key, explaining the persons and places alluded to.

MONTE VIDEO; or the OFFICER'S WIFE and her SISTER. A Novel. By Mrs. BRIDGET BLUEMANTLE.

In 2 vols. 12mo. Price 2 dollars in boards.

VARIETIES OF LIFE; or CONDUCT AND CONSEQUENCES. A Novel in 2 vols. By the Author of "Sketches of Character." Price 2 dollars, in boards.

"If I give speeches and conversations, I ought to give them justly; for the *humours* and *characters* of persons cannot be known, unless I repeat what they say, and their *manner* of saying." *Richardson.*

"We turn with all the elasticity of awakened hope to a second production of the pen of that lively and accurate observer, the Author of "Sketches of Character," a work which has obtained a well-deserved popularity, and is perpetually recurring to the recollection of every person, who, possessing a miscellaneous acquaintance, is in the slightest degree gifted with a talent for the Comedy of Real Life. It is really difficult to imagine how such very dissimilar walks of life, as are depictured in these pages (*Varieties of Life*) can possibly be familiar to one and the same person. From that *gentility* of blood, mind, and manners, in the Ponsonbys, which looks down upon the glare, frivolity and dash of mere fashion, &c. down to the gossip and slang of abigails and valets, all is in its place, all is true to nature." *Augustan Rev.*

JULIA DE ROUBIGNE; a Tale, in a Series of Letters.

By ALEXANDER MACKENZIE,

Author of "Man of Feeling," and "Man of the World." A new edition. To which is added, the Dying Ode of Julia de Roubigne, not inserted in any former edition. With a Frontispiece. In 18mo. Price 63 cents, bound.

MEMOIRS OF AN AMERICAN LADY, with SKETCHES of MANNERS and SCENERY in AMERICA, as they existed previous to the Revolution. In 12mo. Price 1 dollar, boards.

"These letters are written in a superior style, and contain much matter of interest. With touching sensibility the author has pourtrayed the primitive manners of the colonists, and drawn pictures altogether new and delightful." *Lady's Museum.*

"This is a work of very considerable merit." *Aikin's Ann. Rev.*

MONTALBERT. By CHARLOTTE SMITH.

In 2 vols. 12mo, Price 2 dollars, bound.

THE COTTAGE GIRL. By the author of Rosa in London.

In 18mo. Price 63 cents, in boards.

EDUCATION.

NUGENT'S FRENCH AND ENGLISH DICTIONARY.

Second American edition. Price 225 cents, bound.

ENGLISH GRAMMAR, adapted to the different Classes of Learners. With an Appendix, containing Rules and Observations, for assisting the more advanced Students to write with Perspicuity and Accuracy.

By LINDLEY MURRAY.

Stereotype edition. Price 75 cents, bound.

MATERNAL SOLICITUDE FOR A DAUGHTER'S BEST INTERESTS. By Mrs. TAYLOR, of Ongar, Author of "Practical Hints to young Females," &c.

In 12mo. Price 75 cents, boards.

"The subjects of these essays are well chosen and ingeniously diversified, and the fair writer displays a degree of piety, with a knowledge and application of the scripture, which increases the value of her work."

Monthly Review, 1814.

A CLASSICAL DICTIONARY, containing a copious account of all the PROPER NAMES mentioned in ANCIENT AUTHORS; with the value of Coins, Weights and measures, used among the Greeks and Romans; and a Chronological Table.

By J. LEMPRIERE, D. D.

Second American, from the Eighth London Edition.

In 8vo. Price 5 dollars bound.

A CRITICAL PRONOUNCING DICTIONARY, and EXPOSITOR of the ENGLISH LANGUAGE. In which, not only the meaning of every word is clearly explained, and the sound of every word distinctly shown; but, where words are subject to different pronunciations, the authorities of our best Pronouncing Dictionaries are fully exhibited, the reasons for each at large displayed, and the preferable pronunciation pointed out. To which are prefixed, PRINCIPLES of ENGLISH PRONUNCIATION; in which the sounds of letters, syllables, and words, are critically investigated and systematically arranged, &c. &c. &c. The whole interspersed with Observations, Etymological, Critical, and Grammatical.

By JOHN WALKER,

Author of "Elements of Elocution." &c. &c. &c. In 8vo. Price 350 cents, bound, or, on fine paper, 4 dollars bound.

ROMAN ANTIQUITIES; or an Account of the MANNERS and CUSTOMS of the ROMANS, respecting their Government, Magistracy, Laws, Judicial proceedings, Religion, Games, Military and Naval affairs, Dress, Exercises, Baths, Marriages, Divorces, Weights and Measures, Coins, Agriculture, Public Buildings, &c. &c. &c. Designed chiefly to illustrate the Latin Classics, by explaining words and phrases, from the rites and customs to which they refer.

By ALEXANDER ADAM, L. L. D.

Rector of the High School of Edinburgh. In 8vo. Price 3 dollars, bound.

ELLEN; or, the YOUNG GODMOTHER. A Tale,

By ALICIA CATHARINE MANT.

In 18mo. Price 63 cents, half bound, morocco backs.

"When to correct principles and religious tenets, are added a good diction, considerable discrimination, and a well-wrought story, that would not discredit a work destined to higher purposes, and addressed to intellects in a more improved state, nothing more need be said in its favour."

Monthly Museum, April, 1816.

POPULAR MODELS, and IMPRESSIVE WARNINGS, to the Sons and Daughters of Industry. By Mrs. GRANT.

In 2 vols 12mo. Price 150 cents, boards.

"No work published within the last twenty years, has merited more general currency." *Monthly Magazine, May*, 1816.

"It is with sincere pleasure that we embrace the opportunity of noticing a second publication from Mrs. Grant, addressed to "the Sons and Daughters of Industry."

La Belle Assemblee.

A TREATISE OF ALGEBRA. Wherein the principles are demonstrated, and applied to many useful and interesting enquiries, and in the resolution of a great variety of problems of different kinds. To which is added, the Geometrical construction of a great number of Linear and plane problems, with the method of resolving the same numerically.
By THOMAS SIMPSON, F. R. S.
In 8vo. Price 250 cents, bound.

THE PANORAMA OF YOUTH. By MARY STERNDALE. First American, from the 2d London edition. In 2 vols. 12mo.
Price 175 cents half bound, with Morocco backs.

"The tales themselves are written with ability, and their design is meritorious. They conclude with a well-executed allegory, entitled the "Voyage of life;" and the whole production is calculated to stimulate the feelings on the side of virtue." *Mon. Rev.*

SCIENTIFIC DIALOGUES, intended for the instruction and entertainment of young people; in which the first PRINCIPLES of NATURAL and EXPERIMENTAL PHILOSOPHY are explained.
By the Rev. J. JOYCE.
Second American edition. In 3 vols. 18mo, with plates. Price 3 dollars, bound.

A PRESENT for a YOUNG SERVANT; consisting of Friendly Advice and Real Histories. By MRS. TAYLOR, of Ongar, author of "Practical Hints to Young Females," &c. &c.
In 18mo. Price 63 cents, in boards.

"She addresses young servants; and recommends to their practice a behaviour and conduct which cannot fail to insure their respectability." *Literary Panorama.*

"We are happy to announce another publication of this judicious and useful writer, particularly as we think that the present will be found among the most valuable of Mrs. Taylor's productions. The size of the volume is attractive; and the style, though correct, is so unaffected and simple, that every word will be understood by the class of readers for which it is designed." *Monthly Review, March,* 1816.

GEOGRAPHICAL QUESTIONS, adapted to the new Abridgment of MORSE'S GEOGRAPHY; for the use of Schools.
By the Rev. DAVID GRAHAM.
In 12mo. Price 38 cents, half bound.

JOSEPHINE; or the ADVANTAGES OF A SUMMER. A Tale intended for the instruction and amusement of Young Ladies.
In 18mo. Price 50 cents, in boards.

TALES OF THE CASTLE; or STORIES of INSTRUCTION and DELIGHT. Being Les Veillees du Chateau, written in French by
Madame la COMPTESSE DE GENLIS.
and translated into English by THOMAS HOLCROFT. 9th edition.
In 2 vols. 12mo. Price 2 dollars, in boards.

PHILADELPHIA HARMONY; or, a Collection of Psalm Tunes, Hymns, and Anthems, selected by A. ADGATE. Together with the Rudiments of Music on a new and Improved Plan, by A. ADGATE, P. U. A. With an Improved mode of teaching Music, to facilitate the progress of a learner. By JOHN J. HUSBAND.
Price, 1 dollar, half bound.

VISIT FOR A WEEK; or HINTS on the IMPROVEMENT of TIME. Containing, Original Tales, entertaining stories, interesting anecdotes, and sketches from natural and moral history. In 12mo. Price 88 cents, bound.

(3)

A HISTORY OF VIRGINIA, from its discovery till the year 1781. With BIOGRAPHICAL SKETCHES of all the most distinguished characters in the Colonial, Revolutionary, and subsequent period of our History.
By J. W. CAMPBELL.
In 12mo. Price 125 cents, bound.

THE LIFE OF WASHINGTON, with Curious Anecdotes equally honourable to himself, and exemplary to his Young Countrymen.
By the Rev. MASON L. WEEMS.
Seventeenth Edition. Embellished with a Portrait, a Map of the United States, and six Historical Engravings. In 12mo. Price 1 dollar, bound.

"This little volume is designed for an introduction into schools, and as it contains many interesting anecdotes of Washington, and is written in a style very fascinating to the young, it will have an extensive circulation. It has indeed already, in less than two years, passed through eight editions. This is an honourable proof, that the public curiosity is yet awake, in respect to the life and character of the beloved hero of the Revolution.

"It has been a subject of just complaint, that in the lives of Washington, which have appeared, there has been so little of Biography, and so much of history, that we behold him only on the stage of public action, and are not permitted to see him in the private walks of life. Mr. Weems comes forward to supply this deficiency. He has collected a number of facts, particularly relating to the childhood and youth of the American sage, and has presented them to the public, in such an interesting, and frequently comic dress, that it will require the most immoveable gravity of disposition, to preserve a composure of muscles, in reading this book. With this inimitable talent for humour, it is a happy circumstance, that the author has a higher object than a laugh. He perceives the value of religion, and he wishes to recommend it by the example of Washington." *Panoplist and Mis. Mag. united.*

THE ADVENTURES of TELEMACHUS, the Son of ULYSSES. Translated from the French of FENELON, Archbishop of Cambray,
By JOHN HAWKESWORTH.
In 2 vols. 18mo. Price 175 cents, bound.

BUTLER'S GEOGRAPHICAL and MAP EXERCISES. Designed for the use of Young Ladies and Gentlemen. Corrected and improved.
By STEPHEN ADDINGTON.
2d edition. In 12mo. with a 4to. Atlas. Price 113 cents—or, 150 cents, coloured.

"Nothing is so entertaining as Maps." *Lord Chesterfield.*

"In our opinion, there are few writers on the subject of Practical Education, to whom our female offspring are under greater obligations, than to the author of the present work." *Lady's Museum.*

FERGUSON'S LECTURES on SELECT SUBJECTS, in Mechanics, Hydrostatics, Hydraulics, Pneumatics, Optics, Geography, Astronomy, and Dialling. A new edition; corrected and enlarged. With notes and an appendix, adapted to the present state of the Arts and Sciences,
By DANIEL BREWSTER, A. M.
Carefully revised and corrected. By ROBERT PATTERSON, Professor of Mathematics, and Teacher of Natural Philosophy in the University of Pennsylvania. Second American edition. In 2 vols. 8vo. with a volume of plates. Price 7 dollars, bound.

PRINCIPLES OF POLITENESS, and knowing the World.
By the late LORD CHESTERFIELD.
With additions by the Rev. JOHN TRUSLER. Containing every instruction necessary to complete the Gentleman and Man of Fashion—to teach him a knowledge of life, and make him well received in all companies. To which is annexed GREGORY'S LEGACY. For the improvement of youth; but not beneath the attention of any. In 12mo. Price 38 cents, half bound.

PRINTED FOR M. CAREY & SON, PHILADELPHIA.

THE POLITE LADY; or a course of FEMALE EDUCATION: in a series of Letters from a Mother to a Daughter. In 12mo. Price 75 cents, bound.

A NEW ROMAN HISTORY; from the foundation of Rome, to the end of the Commonwealth. With cuts. Designed for the use of Young Ladies and Gentlemen. In 18mo. Price 50 cents, half bound.

THE BROTHER AND SISTER. A Tale, By Mrs. OPIE.
In 18mo. Price 25 cents.

THE HISTORY OF GREECE from the earliest state, to the DEATH of ALEXANDER the GREAT. By Dr. GOLDSMITH.
In 12mo. Price 1 dollar, bound.

A KEY TO BONNYCASTLE'S MENSURATION; containing as plain a solution to every problem and question left unsolved in that Treatise, as the nature of each case can admit. Arranged for the American edition of 1812, with proper references. By THOMAS CROSBIE.
In 12mo. Price 1 dollar, bound.

A COMPENDIOUS EXPOSITOR of English words derived from the Latin, Greek, and French. By J. GOUGH, S. M.
4th edition improved, with the addition of nearly 1000 words not in any former one. In 12mo. Price 25 cents, half bound.

THE UNIVERSAL LETTER WRITER; or the whole ART of POLITE CORRESPONDENCE. Containing a great variety of plain, easy, entertaining, and familiar original Letters, adapted to every age and situation in Life, but more particularly on BUSINESS, EDUCATION and LOVE. To which is added, a modern collection of Genteel complimentary cards. Likewise useful forms in Law, such as Bonds, Wills, &c.
In 12mo. Price 50 cents, half bound.

GURNEY'S easy and Compendious SYSTEM of SHORT HAND; adapted to the Arts and Sciences, and to the learned professions. Improved by THOMAS SERGEANT. 3d American Edition. In 12mo. Price 150 cents, bound.

HISTORY OF PAMELA; or VIRTUE REWARDED. Abridged from the works of SAMUEL RICHARDSON, Esq. In 18mo. Price 25 cents.

THE PARENTS' FRIEND; or EXTRACTS from the PRINCIPAL WORKS on EDUCATION, from the time of Montaigne to the present day, methodized and arranged. With observations and notes.
By RICHARD LOVEL EDGEWORTH, and MARIA EDGEWORTH.
In 2 vols. 8vo. Price 4 dollars, bound.

DILWORTH'S NEW GUIDE to the ENGLISH TONGUE. Price 19 cents.—133 cents per doz.

D. JUNII JUVENALIS et A. PERSII FLACCI SATIRÆ. Interpretatione ac Notis illustravit Ludovicus Prateus, Rhetoricæ professor Emeritus; jussu Christianissimi Regis, in usum Serenissimi Delphini. Editio prima Americana. In 8vo. Price 275 cents, bound.

AN ABRIDGMENT of the HISTORY of ENGLAND from the invasion of Julius Cæsar, to the Death of George the Second.
By Dr. GOLDSMITH,
and continued by an eminent writer to the PEACE OF AMIENS, A. D. 1802. In 12mo. Price 1 dollar, bound.

HISTORY of an OFFICER'S WIDOW, and her young Family.
By Mrs. HOFLAND,
Author of "Son of a Genius," "Ellen, the Teacher," &c. &c. In 18mo. Price 63 cents, in boards.

"The story is interesting, and such as may in a peculiar manner beneficially engage the attention of juvenile minds." *Mon. Rev.*

PABLO y VIRGINIA. Por JACOBO BERNARDINO HENRIQUE de St. PIERRE. Traducido en Espanol por Don JOSEF MIGUEL DE ALEA. In 18mo. Price, 50 cents, half bound.

LECTEUR FRANCOIS; ou Recueil de Pieces, en Prose et en Vers, tirees des Meilleurs Ecrivains. Pour servir a perfectionner les jeunes Gens dans la Lecture; a etendre leur Connoissance de la Langue Francoise; et a leur inculquer des principes de Vertu et de Piete.

Par LINDLEY MURRAY.

Second edition. In 12mo. Price 125 cents, bound.

"Special care has been taken to render the study of eloquence subservient to virtue, and to introduce only such pieces as shall answer the double purpose of promoting good principles, and a correct and elegant taste. This will no doubt be found a very useful school-book." *Mon. Rev.*

"The student will find his advantage in making use of this work, as he will be sure to form his taste after the most correct models." *Crit. Rev.*

LES ADVENTURES de TELEMAQUE, Fils d'Ulysse. Par FENELON. Nouvelle edition, revue et corrigee.

Par M. CHARLES Le BRUN.

In 12mo. Price, 138 cents.

LES ADVENTURES DE TELEMAQUE, fils d'Ulysse.

Par M. FR. DE SALIGNAC DE LA MOTHE FENELON, Archeveque de Cambray. En Francois et en Anglois. Seconde edition Americaine, soigneusement comparee avec les meilleures editions Francoises, revue et corrigee par L. C. VALLON, Professeur de la Langue Francois en l'Universite de Pennsylvanie. In 2 vols. 12mo. Price 225 cents, bound.

ELEMENS de la GRAMMAIRE FRANCOISE, Par M. L'HOMOND. Professeur emerite en la ci-devant Universite de Paris. Dixieme edition.

In 12mo. Price 50 cents, half bound.

Le DIRECTEUR DES ENFANS, depuis l'age de Cinq ans, jusqu 'a douze. Contenant 1. l'Abecedaire, 2. Des Prieres et des meditations Chretiennes, 3. Un examen de Conscience pour l'enfance, 4. Un Catechisme, et des prieres pour la Confession, 5. Un petit traite d'Arithmetique, 6. Des Lectures interessantes, et un recueil choisi de contes et de fables. Nouvelle edition, redige,

Par M. C. LE BRUN.

price on fine paper, half bound, 50 cents,—Common paper 38 cents.

COLUMBIAN SPELLING AND READING BOOK, improved. Price 25 cents.—2 dollars per doz.

La GALATEA de MIGUEL de CERVANTES, imitada, compendiada, concluida por M. FLORIAN. Traducido por D. CASIANO PELLICER. In 18mo. Price 50 cents, half bound.

EL DIRECTOR DE LOS NINOS para aprender a Deletrear; o Metodo para facilitar los progresos de los Ninos quando se mandan par la primera vez ala Escuela. In 18mo. Price 50 cents, half bound.

La PAISANA VIRTUOSA. In 18mo. Price 50 cents, half bound.

Les ELEMENS de la LANGUE ANGLOISE, developpes d'une maniere nouvelle, facile, et tres-concise. Par J. V. PEYTON.

In 12mo. Price 63 cents, half bound.

HOMERI ILIAS, Græce et Latine. Annotationes in usum serenissimi principis Gulielmi Augusti, Ducis de Cumberland, &c. regio jussu scripsit atque edidit SAMUEL CLARKE, S. T. P. Editio prima Americana. Cura GEORGIO IRONSIDE, A. M.

In 2 vols. 8vo. Price 7 dollars, bound.

PRINTED FOR M. CAREY & SON, PHILADELPHIA.

LA PRESUMIDA ORGULLOSA. Por Don ATANASIO CESPEDES y MONROY. In 18mo. Price 50 cents, half bound.

QUINTI HORATII FLACCI OPERA; in Usum Serenissimi Delphini. A new edition, in which many of the errors of the London edition have been corrected. In 8vo. Price 350 cents, bound.

JUSTINUS DE HISTORIIS PHILIPPICIS, et totius mundi originibus. Interpretatione et notis illustravit PETRUS JOSEPHUS CANTEL, E Societate Jesu; Jussu Christianissimi Regis, in usum Serenissimi Delphini. Editio Prima Americana. Accessere JACOBI BONGARSII Excerptiones Chronologicæ, ad Justini historias accommodatæ.
In 8vo. Price 275 cents, bound.

C. JULII CÆSARIS, quæ extant, interpretatione et notis illustravit JOHANNES GODVINUS, professor Regis, in usum Delphini. The notes and interpretations translated and improved
By THOMAS CLARK. In 8vo. Price 250 cents, bound.

CORNELII NEPOTIS, Vitæ Excellentium imperatorum Versione Anglicana, in qua verbum de verbo quantum fieri potuit, redditur: Notisquoque Anglicis et indice locupletissimo; or, CORNELIUS NEPOS'S LIVES of the excellent Commanders, with an English translation as literal as possible, with English notes and a large index. By JOHN CLARKE.
In 12mo. Price 1 dollar, bound.

EPICTETI ENCHIRIDION. Ex editione JOHANNIS UPTON, accurate expressum. In 18mo. Price 31 cents, bound.

THE PHILADELPHIA VOCABULARY, English and Latin: proper to acquaint the learner with things, as well as pure Latin words. Adorned with 26 pictures. For the use of Schools. By JAMES GREENWOOD.
In 12mo. Price 50 cents, bound.

QUINTI HORATII FLACCI OPERA. Ad optimas editiones collata.
In 18mo. Price 1 dollar, bound.

SELECTÆ E PROFANIS SCRIPTORIBUS HISTORIÆ. Quibus admista sunt varia honeste vivendi Præcepta, ex iisdem scriptoribus deprompta. Hæc editio Philadelphiensis prioribus certe emendatior et juventuti utilior. Accurante JA. ROSS.
In 12mo. Price 1 dollar, bound.

CORDERII COLLOQUIORUM CENTURIA Selecta: or, a select Century of the Colloquies of Corderius, with an English translation, as literal as possible; designed for the use of beginners in the Latin tongue.
By JOHN CLARKE.
A new edition, corrected and improved, by JAMES ROSS, Professor of the Latin and Greek Languages in Philadelphia.
In 12mo. Price 50 cents, bound.

SELECTÆ e VETERI TESTAMENTO, queis nonnullæ ex APOCRYPHIS, sive libris incertæ originis, et auctoritatis humanæ, adduntur, HISTORIÆ, ad usum eorum qui Latinæ linguæ rudimentis imbuuntur—editio nova Philadelphiensis, qua signa quantitatis certis syllabis perspicue notantur JA. ROSS, Humaniorum Literarum et Græcæ Linguæ Professore accurante. In 12mo. Price 50 cents, bound.

DESIDERII ERASMI Roterodami colloquia familiaria nonnulla selecta: or some select familiar Colloquies of D. ERASMUS of Rotterdam. With a literal Translation. By JOHN CLARKE.
A new edition, in which many of the errors of former editions (both in the text and translation) have been corrected, and the signs of quantity, to assist the students in pronouncing, are annexed. By JAMES ROSS, Professor of the Greek and Latin Languages in Philadelphia.
In 12mo. Price 50 cents, bound.

Zeitfracht Medien GmbH
Ferdinand-Jühlke-Straße 7
99095 Erfurt, Deutschland
produktsicherheit@kolibri360.de